CATHEDRAL AND UNIVERSITY
SERMONS

CATHEDRAL
AND UNIVERSITY
SERMONS

By GEORGE SALMON, D.D., F.R.S.

PROVOST OF TRINITY COLLEGE, DUBLIN
AND CHANCELLOR OF ST PATRICK'S
CATHEDRAL, DUBLIN

SECOND EDITION

LONDON
JOHN MURRAY, ALBEMARLE STREET
1901

CONTENTS

Contents

SERMON XX

SCRUPLES OF CONSCIENCE

" If any of them that believe not bid you to a feast, and ye
be disposed to go : whatsoever is set before you, eat,
asking no question for conscience sake. But if any
man say unto you, this is offered in sacrifice unto
idols, eat not for his sake that shewed it, and for
conscience sake."—1 COR. x. 27, 28   247

SERMON XXI

THE DAYS OF OUR FATHERS

" We have heard with our ears O God, our fathers have
told us what Thou hast done in their time of old :
how Thou hast driven out the heathen with Thine
hand and planted them in : how Thou hast destroyed
the nations and cast them out."—PSALM xliv. 1, 2   .   262

SERMON I

CHRIST'S REWARD FOR FAITHFUL SERVICE

"And the night following the Lord stood by him, and said, Be of good cheer, Paul: for as thou hast testified of Me in Jerusalem, so must thou bear witness also at Rome."
—ACTS xxiii. 11.

IN the text we have the reward bestowed by our Lord for a bold confession of His name. Our Lord had promised a reward for every good deed done for His sake: even a cup of cold water given to a disciple for love to Him was not to go without its reward. I daresay you will think that no one deserved such reward better than St Paul. I suppose it would be hard to name any one who loved Christ better than St Paul, or was willing to sacrifice more for His sake. He had told the elders of Ephesus that the Holy Ghost had witnessed in every city, saying that bonds and afflictions were abiding him. "But," said he, "none of these things move me, neither count I my life dear unto myself, so that I might finish my course with joy, and the ministry, which I have received of the Lord Jesus, to testify the Gospel of the grace of God." And accordingly, soon after, when he had received a prophetic warning that the Jews would bind him and deliver him into the hands of

A   1

the Gentiles, and when his friends therefore implored him not to go to Jerusalem, he answered : "What mean ye, to weep and to break my heart ? For I am ready not to be bound only, but also to die at Jerusalem for the name of the Lord Jesus." All the apprehensions of his friends were realised. The Jews at Jerusalem set upon him in the temple, beat him, and would have killed him, if the Roman soldiers had not rescued him, though with great difficulty. The next day he was brought before the council of the Jewish elders, where he gave rise to so hot a conflict, that the chief captain, fearing he should be pulled in pieces, sent down his soldiers to deliver him out of their hands. It was the night after all this suffering and danger that our Lord appeared to him with a promise of reward : "Be of good cheer, Paul, for as thou hast testified of Me in Jerusalem, so shalt thou bear witness also in Rome."

The Greek word for "witness" has passed into our English language, where we all know it in the form "martyr." A martyr means no more than a witness for Christ—one who bears faithful testimony, though to the loss of liberty or life. Fully in this sense did Paul bear witness at Rome. He went there, not, as he had once planned, as a missionary on his way to a further self-chosen field of labour, but as a captive bound by a chain to the soldier who guarded him, destined there to suffer a tedious imprisonment, and ultimately, after witnessing a good confession before the tyrant emperor, to die as a martyr, in our English sense of the word.

What! we may ask, Is this the reward Christ has to bestow on His faithful servants ? Are these His compensations for toil and suffering at Jerusalem—more toil, more suffering at Rome? Is the reward for buffeting and imprisonment borne for Christ's sake no better than a worse imprisonment and a martyr's death? Nay, what is the reward which in God's ordinary government of the world He bestows on those who have done good work? None higher than the power to do other work of the same kind more easily, and to do it better. What reward that he would have valued more highly could you have bestowed on St Paul if the distribution of rewards had rested with you? Is it money? Would you think of offering it to him who could say that he had suffered the loss of all things, and did count them but dung, that he might win Christ? Is it honour? Well, honour he has had. All over the civilised world his name is kept in memory. It is enough to remind you how, annually, his memory is specially honoured by us, the inhabitants of an island so remote, and regarded as so outside the pale of civilisation, that with all the apostle's eagerness to plant the standard of the Gospel in new lands, he never seems to have planned to pay it a visit, but to have thought that he should reach the very boundary of the Western world if he could make Christ known in Spain.

Yet who can imagine Paul's work as prompted by a desire to win the praise of men? If that were his ambition it was but little gratified in his lifetime. He did, indeed, win the enthusiastic affection of a small number of attached disciples; but, on the other hand, he was pursued by the bitter hatred of the great body of his countrymen, who scorned and loathed him as an apostate, as one that had deserted the chosen people to consort with the uncircumcised ; while from the Roman rulers he sometimes met contemptuous toleration ; sometimes, if so paltry a sacrifice could advance the personal interests of the governor, he was delivered over to the malice of his enemies.

But, in truth, if Paul's work had been prompted by desire to gain glory, or any other advantage for himself, it was impossible that he could have accomplished it. His work was to inspire in others love for Christ, and he succeeded in doing it, because love for Christ was the chief animating principle of his whole life, being such that his sole desire was, as he said himself, "that Christ should be magnified by him, whether by life or by death." What earthly reward would not have seemed to him wretchedly poor in comparison with the knowledge that his work was approved by Him for whom it was done ? Even in things of this life, that is the only kind of honour that is valued by one who does his work well. What good workman cares much for the praise of people who don't know good work from bad ? If in the course of a campaign an officer had successfully performed some service entrusted to him, he might, perhaps, be pleased if a newspaper correspondent gave a flattering account of his performance, giving him some praise that he deserved, and some more that, perhaps, he very well knew he did not ; but what would that honour be in comparison with this, that the next time the commander-in-chief wanted some service done of unusual danger and difficulty, he picked him out as the man above all others likely to do it successfully ? Danger or difficulty there might be, but what would these be in comparison with the honour? This comparison accurately represents the character of the service demanded from St Paul, and justifies me in regarding the being entrusted with the commission as the highest reward for his past labours that his Master could have bestowed on him. Since the Ascension of our Lord there has been no such important epoch in the history of our religion as that which was indicated in the words: "As thou hast borne witness of Me in Jerusalem, so shalt thou bear witness also in Rome." It was the change of the centre of operations of the Christian preachers from Jerusalem, the capital of the Jewish nation, to Rome, which was then beyond dispute the capital of the world. The move decided that Christianity was not to be a mere sect of Judaism, but a world-religion. You can easily appreciate the immense importance of the change, and will readily own that, compared with being the instrument in making it, no work done by any other Christian missionary deserves to be mentioned. But if the service was an important one, it was also one of difficulty and danger. The difficulty, indeed, was appalling, and, before the event, might well have seemed insurmountable: difficulty arising from exclusive pride on the one side, scorn and hatred on the other. How did it seem possible to bring together as brethren at the same table the Jew, who thought it pollution to eat with the uncircumcised, and the Roman, who felt angry contempt for the slave that dared to think himself superior to his masters, and who, while tolerant of all other religions, hated the intolerance of these bigoted provincials, who refused a share in any of the good offices of life to

men outside their pale? As for danger, Paul's summary of his experience may suffice: " In perils of
waters, in perils of robbers, in perils by mine own
countrymen, in perils by the heathen, in perils in the
city, in perils in the wilderness, in perils in the sea, in
perils among false brethren." Yet the success was
complete, and Paul lived to see it; and when he
looked round on the number of Gentile churches
which claimed him as their founder, he could not for-
bear expressing his thankfulness, mixed with wonder,
that God should have chosen him to make known to
him the mystery which, in other ages, had not been
made known to the sons of men—that the Gentiles
should be fellow-heirs and of the same Body,—and
had employed him, though " less than the least of all
saints, to preach among the Gentiles the unsearchable
riches of Christ" (Ephes. iii. 8).

I have already said how the memory of the great
work done by the apostle Paul has been honoured in
every Christian Church. But I must now add that
unbelievers, even more than Christians, have been
struck by the greatness of his achievement in so
modifying the ideas of the original apostles as to fit
their religion for becoming the faith of the world.
There have been those who profess to regard Paul,
and not Jesus, as the real founder of Christianity.
Others, in more recent times, who have professed to
write the life of Paul, have represented him as having,
by his private meditation, thought out the whole plan
immediately on his first conversion, and as having
commenced his work by preaching to the Gentiles at
a time when no one was prepared for such a work,
and when, by doing so, Paul would have put himself

in a position of complete isolation, hated alike by the Jews, whom he left, and by the Christian society to which he wished to join himself. It is very common with those who trace the history of the career of men who have raised themselves to great and unexpected distinction, to imagine them as having in early life planned for themselves the position they were ultimately to reach, and as having all their life schemed to secure it. But in real life the ambitious dreams of the young man seldom get beyond the stage of castle-building. The men who succeed are practical men, who, perhaps, have never sketched out to themselves beforehand what the course of events is to be, but who promptly take advantage of every opening that actual circumstances offer. If it were asked, how came Paul to divine that, while the Jews, with all the advantage of having the prophetic Scriptures in their hands, refused to recognise Jesus as " He of whom Moses in the Law and the Prophets did write," the Gentiles would be found disposed to acknowledge His Messiahship, we need not imagine, as some have done, that this was the result of profound meditation on his part on all that was implied in the preaching of One who had been crucified ; nor do I think we need imagine more than Scripture has told us of special revelations of God to him. Whatever his own feelings or wishes might have been, a Providential Hand was guiding him. How is it that water dammed up will contrive to make its way through a barrier which might seem impenetrable? It is that by its continuous pressure against the obstacle, it explores it all, until its searching has found some weak part. If such there be, and even a minute stream manages to trickle through, as the tiny flow proceeds the orifice constantly enlarges itself, more and more of the opposing barrier crumbles away, the stream becomes a torrent, and at length, with resistless force, carries all before it. Such a pressure as I have described was exercised by that love for Christ, of which Paul's heart was full, and which constantly urged him to seek others to whom to impart it. Disappointed he must have been to find that the men of his own race and religion, with whom, when he was zealous for the law, his influence had been the greatest, were too hardened by life-long prejudice to yield any admission to the new teaching. Meanwhile, it would be a surprise to find that fit audience could be found among the despised few who fringed the circle of his Jewish hearers—proselytes, curious listeners, who had come to hear what went on in the Jewish Synagogue. Surprising it might seem to him, yet quite natural to us. These men had already lost their faith in the outworn creeds in which they had been brought up, full of childish fables, which could neither satisfy the intellect nor touch the heart. In the lofty monotheism of the Jews they could not but recognise something far superior to the popular beliefs of their countrymen. Yet for their adopted creed they had not the long-grown bigoted attachment of those who had been brought up in it. As they had owned its superiority to what their childhood had learned, so they were open to accept something still higher if it were presented to them. In their ranks, then, the Gospel message found the weak spot in the opposing barrier. First one, then another, would consent to acknowledge Jesus as his Lord. Every new convert would be a centre of influence on his friends and countrymen; the little trickle became a stream. The converts were so numerous that the question became an urgent one, which cost Paul a few years of distressing controversy: what conditions were to be imposed on the new disciples; must they be circumcised and observe the Mosaic Law? until at length, and mainly by Paul's exertions, the wall of partition which divided Jew from Gentile was completely swept away, and it became acknowledged by all that in Christ Jesus there was neither Jew nor Gentile, circumcision or uncircumcision, but Christ was all and in all.

I have dwelt on the gradual process by which the apostle of the Gentiles was educated for his work, because of the practical lesson for ourselves, who live under the same law of God's government of the world which was exemplified in the words to him: "As thou hast borne witness in Jerusalem, so shalt thou bear witness also in Rome." Still the rule is: "To him that hath shall more be given." We need not expect a special revelation making known to us the work God has for us to do. The little duty that lies in our way, if faithfully discharged, both trains ourselves in the power to do something more difficult, leads others to trust us with something more difficult, and educates our own eye to take notice of neglected opportunities, and see what ought to be done, and which, if no one else will do it, there seems a necessity that we should undertake to do. Of those who enter on a new sphere of duty there are some, no doubt, who have observed beforehand unnoticed capabilities in it, and have begun with the expectation of doing more in it than any one before them had done. But there are many more who are led on by little and little, and would have been frightened, as well as surprised, if it could have been told them beforehand that it was expected that they should do all that in the event came naturally to them. Put your best into all the work that God gives you, and you will find yourself led on to more and higher work, and will one day hear His words: "Well done, good and faithful servant: thou hast been faithful in a few things, I will make thee ruler over many things."

SERMON II

THE PARTING OF THE WAYS

"But what, is thy servant a dog, that he should do this great thing?"—2 KINGS viii. 13.

SUCH is the form in which the Authorised Version gives the answer of the Syrian Captain, Hazael, when Elisha predicted to him the evil that he would one day do to the Jewish nation; how he would set their strongholds on fire, slay their young men with the sword, dash their children, and rip up their women with child. And the answer has been commonly understood, as if Hazael, struck with horror at the announcement, repelled the idea that he could ever be dog enough to commit such enormities. But careful readers have felt that it would not cause a Syrian much distress to be told of the victories which his country was to gain over a rival people; and at a time when conquerors had no scruple to exact to the full the penalties which the vanquished had to pay, the recital of what were then the ordinary incidents of warfare would not give the shock which is felt by the sensitiveness of modern humanity. The triumphs of his country had probably been long the subject of Hazael's meditations; and what had most interest for

him in the prophet's prediction was that these
triumphs were to be gained by one so mean as, in real
or affected modesty, he is willing to describe himself.
And so the Revised Version translates his answer:
"But what is thy servant, which is but a dog, that *he*
should do this great thing."

For my present purpose the double interpretation
that has been put on the text by our two versions is
convenient, because I am about to speak of the
development of character in the progress of life, a
development which often gives surprises in both
directions. Some of whom we had thought but
meanly, exhibit, when occasion demands it, fine
qualities for which we had not given them credit, and
perform actions of which we had not thought them
capable; while, again, with some, whose early years
had given promise of an honourable future, our expectations are disappointed: the principles that at
the first had guided their conduct seem to fade away,
and if, in their ingenuous youth, some of their later
actions could have been predicted to them, they would
have been tempted to reply in Hazael's words, feeling
it an insult that it should be imagined they could
ever do such things.

In fact, it is in the law of nature that seeds give little
indication of their innate potentialities. Not only is
the seed surprisingly unlike the mature growth, a fact
noted in one of our Lord's parables, where He con-
trasts the tiny seed with the great tree that springs
from it, in the branches whereof the birds of the air
come to lodge; but seeds of quite different plants
have so much general resemblance, that an in-
experienced person who had only seen the full-

grown plants would be baffled if he attempted to assign to which each seed belonged.

And, again, it is not only that seeds give no indication of what is to spring from them, but even the early growth exhibits little token of its future. Of two babes smiling in their mothers' arms, the one may be destined by the vigour of his body and the strength of his intellect to raise himself to sovereign power, and command the obedience of thousands; and yet this born ruler of men has not yet come into possession of his birthright; he rules, not thousands of men, but one woman; and her he rules by his weakness, his feeble wail being more sure to obtain service than the sternest order he may afterwards issue in the days of his power. The other babe might live to be infamous for his crimes, and, to exemplify the truth of the proverb, "A foolish son is the heaviness of his mother." Yet in his infant days he, as much as the other, is her delight, and the joy with which she smiles on him is not alloyed by any foreboding of the bitter tears he may one day cause her to shed.

If we ask the ancient question, whether the different results in different cases arise from nature or education, we must admit that both factors have to be taken into account; but if we look at the subject, not from a speculative, but from a practical point of view, we find that far the more important is "education," understanding that word, in a large sense, to include all the influences that surrounding circumstances exercise in the shaping of character. If we were only concerned with theory, we should give the first place to nature, which has given a considerable amount of plasticity to the constitutions of living organisms, and yet has put certain limits on their modifications. We cannot expect by any amount of cultivation to get figs from thistles, or to find a bramble-bush bringing forth grapes. Thus, though the question of the possibility of a transformation of species is a highly interesting one from the point of view of scientific history, we know that as a practical question we must limit our expectations of producing change by culture, by the condition that the change shall take place within the bounds of what we commonly call the same species. And we must own that even within the same species capacities are diverse; that some are capable of higher developments than others; that some have to contend with temptations from which others are comparatively free. It would lead me too far away from my subject if I were now to discuss the causes of these diversities; though the question of heredity is not one of merely scientific interest, it has a deeply practical side. It is well that we should know that the penalties on wrong-doing are far greater than we might have imagined. It is not only that each step we take on the downward road makes our own recovery more difficult; that habits are formed, the chains of which we find it hard to break when we are longing and struggling to be free; but the evil that we do lives after us, lives in descendants who, through our sins, are condemned with impaired strength to encounter fiercer temptations. But though, as I have said, the question of heredity has more than a speculative scientific interest, yet what we are practically concerned with is only the things that lie within our own power. It profits little to enquire why we have not been born with greater powers. Such as we are, we are; and even if it be the fault of our ancestors that we do not start in life's race with greater advantages, the fact remains that if we do wrong it is we who must pay the penalty. For practical purposes the really important truth is, that such as we are, we are not bound to remain. The powers given us may be improved; the disadvantages under which we start may be overcome, and thus, as the text intimates, so great a change may be made that we could scarce believe it if it had been predicted to us. What profit is there to complain that others have been entrusted with ten talents and we only with five, when the fact is that it is possible for us to improve our five talents into ten?

I daresay I shall be thought to say a paradoxical thing if I express my belief that young men in general have too poor an opinion of themselves, and, like Hazael, have too little faith in what it is in their power to become. I use the word "faith," because I want to exclude a kind of belief or flattering persuasion on which they have no courage to act. Castle-building is pleasant. When the greater part of the pages in the book of life are still blank, it is delightful to imagine what fine things may one day be written in them. The maiden may dream of the prince who will one day come and find in her face attractions greater than her glass can at present give her assurance of. And on whatever hero the young man has fixed his admiration, it is a cheap pleasure to him to imagine himself rivalling or outdoing that hero's greatest feats. Yet while he is indulging in those dreams of fancied victory in the race, he has not yet entered for it, much less begun to train for it. One reason, perhaps, is that he has a consciousness that if he put his powers to the test he should be likely to find a humiliating contrast between what he wished might be and what he should actually find them to be. Queen Elizabeth's courtier wrote : " Fain would I climb, but that I fear to fall." Many a one has sunk into inactivity, the combined result of a pride that would not brook defeat, and a self-knowledge that defeat was not impossible. Perhaps on measuring strength with contemporaries he has found himself inferior, and prefers therefore not to compete at all, rather than accept something lower than that first place, which alone would satisfy his ambition. It is a feature perfectly true to life that in our Lord's parable the only servant who has made absolutely no profit on his master's trust is he to whom but one talent had been committed. *That* he thought too small to be worth improving. And so I come back to what I said, that a common cause of failure in life (if in the word failure we include the attainment of a much lower position than might have been successfully gained) is too low a real opinion of one's powers, combined with a shrinking from exposure to others that this low opinion of ours is a true one.

Yet it is a cowardly thing to shrink from combat through fear of defeat. Defeat is commonly the discipline by which victory is prepared. Few are so happily constituted as to be able to gain success on a first attempt. The experience of the majority is trial followed by failure, in some cases disgraceful failure ; then, with errors corrected by experience, trial again ; it may be, failure again. And when at length success comes, it is recognised that, but for the lessons learned in the school of disappointment, the victory could not have been won.

Yet I shall seem to counsel ill if my advice is taken to be, to fix our ambitions high, and never tarry to calculate whether the mark we aim at is above our reach or not. Yet I do believe that, if I even were so understood, the harm done by my advice would be comparatively small. I have seen so many cases in which strenuous effort has been rewarded by unexpected development of powers, that I am persuaded that the disappointment of too lofty ambition is far more rare than the shortcomings of indolent contentment with a low level. But of course I am not so foolish as to counsel the injudicious expenditure of strength on work for which we are not suited. The ways of doing good work in the world are infinitely various, and it is only common-sense to direct our energies into those channels to which our tastes incline us, or in which trial shows us that we have most prospects of success.

Indeed the advice, " Fix your ambitions high," though capable of a very good sense, is one that much needs an interpreter ; for it might easily mislead if misunderstood. Probably it would be less dangerous advice to say : " Have no ambition ; " or, in the words of the prophet Jeremiah, " Seekest thou great things for thyself, seek them not." It does occasionally happen in the case of some exceptionally gifted men, that in early life they become conscious that there is a work which needs to be done, and which they feel courage to undertake, though it might seem to be above their strength, and undertake it rather for the sake of the work than for credit to be gained by themselves. I don't see why I should not name one case that occurs to me, that of a dear friend of my own, the Cambridge astronomer, Professor Adams. It had been suspected before that the irregularities of the motions of Uranus, the exterior of the then known planets, might possibly be caused by the attraction of an unknown planet still more remote; but no one had seen how to bring this suspicion to the test of calculation. Adams, while still an under-graduate, had resolved to grapple with the problem as soon as he had obtained his degree; and when the time came he did so successfully, determining the place of a planet whose presence would account for the observed irregularities. No one was more free from personal ambition, and it was well that this had not been the motive that actuated him, for if so, he would have experienced a severe disappointment. The story is well known. The leading English astronomer who had been requested to search for the new planet in the predicted place, unable to believe that an unknown young man had performed so unprecedented a feat, could not persuade himself to give serious attention to the imagined discovery; and meanwhile the glory of the first announcement was obtained by a continental astronomer, who, as sometimes strangely happens, had simultaneously attacked the same problem, and had been more fortunate in finding a skilled observer willing to believe in him. Yet the English mathematician felt the disappointment far less acutely than did others interested in the fame of his country and university. And that his indifference was not affected, is proved by the whole tenor of his life of quiet work in which the *fallentis semita vitæ* seemed fully to content his ambition. Contrasted with this, I think of others whom I have known, who, on entering on the work of manhood felt a burning desire to distinguish themselves by making some great discovery, they cared not much what. But since, unfortunately, it is not true that every one who digs will find a nugget, their labour was rewarded by what they regarded as very inadequate returns.

The question has been discussed whether such men as Cæsar or Cromwell or Napoleon did not, at the very outset of their respective careers, set before themselves the position to which they ultimately attained, and thenceforward direct all their conduct with the view of arriving at it. It is needless to discuss what answer is to be given to this question in the cases I have named; for certain it is that the ambition of extremely few is so far-sighted; and wisely so, for the most likely result of fixing the gaze on a distant object would be to miss taking advantage of opportunities just lying under our feet. The ordinary history of a successful career is that it begins with a comparatively humble task, faithfully and well performed, and that the successful performance of this task both gives to the young man himself courage to undertake a more difficult one, and gives others confidence to entrust him with it. "*Mox in ovilia; nunc in reluctantes dracones.*" In the interests, then, of ambition itself, I might caution you against premature ambitions; against undertaking work, neither from love of the work itself, nor in obedience to any call of duty, but from a desire

for self-exaltation, which brings with it the temptation to rush at feats for the successful performance of
which there has been no adequate training. As
a general rule, far better results are obtained by the
man who has had little thought of self, but who has
followed the rule, " Whatsoever thy hand findeth to do,
do it with thy might," not scorning a too humble task
as if it were not worth doing, not deterred by fear of
failure from afterwards entering on a more difficult
one if it appeared that there was a due call on him to
undertake it.[1]   It is such men as these who earn the
Master's commendation : " Well done, thou good and
faithful servant : thou has been faithful over a few
things, I will make thee ruler over many things."

Thus far I have only dwelt on the thoughts that
arise from one aspect of the text, and have spoken of
the display by men, when occasion arises, of powers
unsuspected even by themselves.   But there is a
darker side to the picture at which it would not
be right that we should refuse to look.   The law
of life is evolution.   Living creatures do not at first
come into being with the characters and powers
which they are ultimately to exhibit.   To take notice
of the development of new powers is but to witness
the ordinary course of nature.   But what is just
as much the course of nature, though it does not
equally force itself on our attention, is the loss by
living creatures of unused powers.   No comparison
with inanimate objects will express by a parable the
fact that a man who buries his talent in a napkin,
if he should repent, and afterwards desire to use

[1] We had lately a signal illustration of such a career in the history
of the statesman, W. H. Smith.

it, will not find it there. This fading of unused powers is one of the causes why it is so difficult to maintain a stationary position. Not to advance is to recede, the case having been truly compared to that of a man whose task it is to urge a boat against the course of a descending stream; if he chance to relax his efforts, he is rapidly borne downward by the current. Yet in how many cases do we see powers go to waste, not from any deliberate contempt of the work, such as I have warned you against, but from the superior attractions of pleasures, or it may be of mere indolence. And then not only do powers decay, but the law of growth and evolution again comes into play. For in neglected fields springs up the weed, fit but for the fire; and weeds will grow and multiply at least as rapidly as the useful plant, and the result is what the wise man describes : "I went by the field of the slothful, and by the vineyard of the man void of understanding; and, lo, it was all grown over with thorns, and nettles had covered the face thereof, and the stone wall thereof was broken down."

The worst of it is that however dismal the aspect of the field might now appear to a stranger's eye, the growth of weeds has been silent, and almost unmarked by the owner. Duties neglected, the discharge of them daily put off to a more convenient season, and at length utterly forgotten; suggestions of conscience disregarded, and her voice at length silenced; good principles, through not being acted on, ceasing to have any influence, result in a deterioration of character, which the sufferer would one day not have believed, if it could have been predicted to him. For there is a double impulse on the downward road, as habit adds force to temptations which have been yielded to, and removes counter-checks which it seems useless to oppose to a stronger force when they have been found powerless against a weaker.

It has been cynically said, there comes a time in people's lives when they get tired of being virtuous; and no doubt, if this is represented as a general experience, it is grossly untrue; yet one constantly sees cases of men who yield in middle life to temptations which they have overcome in youth. For though the temptations of youth are strong, yet in the case of those who have had the happiness of being brought up in virtue and piety, the forces of resistance are stronger. There is a felt impossibility of breaking rules which we have been trained from childhood to reverence; there is the dread of losing the good opinion of men whose esteem we value— nay, with the tempter's appeal is heard an answering cry: "How can I do this great wickedness and sin against GOD?" But as years go on, the rules learned in youth lose something of their authority. We fall into the society of persons who disregard them. Some of the restrictions we had in youth to submit to appear to our mature judgment arbitrary and unwise; others we have yielded to the temptation of breaking, and, by dint of breaking them, have trained our conscience to make no remonstrance; and as the consciousness of matured strength disposes us to take our own way, and care less for the judgment of others, the temptation becomes stronger to please self at all hazards, and to grasp at attainable objects of desire, indifferent to the disapprobation we shall incur.

Thus as life goes on, the features of our moral character alter as much as those of our physical form ; and if it were possible that the vigorous youth could be shown a photograph of the broken-down old man he is one day to become, he might not be more disposed to deny all resemblance than he would be to disclaim identity with the moral wreck which his after life might exhibit.

It would have been very unpractical to spend time in representing to you the possibilities that lie before you in the unknown future, if it were not that for you who stand at the parting of the ways, it is important to know that, though you cannot tell how far in either direction you will ultimately advance, it is still in your power to choose which direction you will take. Among all the productions of heathen literature, none seems to have had more attraction for early Christian writers than the apologue which Xenophon has preserved for us of the choice of Hercules. The story is probably known to you all. It told how, when the hero was entering on manhood, he was met by two women, each of whom invited him to be her companion. The one promised that if he would go with her, he should be asked to undertake no toils and encounter no danger ; he should be lapped in the softest of pleasures, and be denied no gratification which his desires might crave. The other taught him the price at which these promises were to be gained : that of never hearing the sweetest sound—that of praise deserved ; never seeing the sweetest sight—that of a good work of which yourself have been the doer. She did not conceal that she was asking him to climb a long and toilsome steep, but she assured him that it was only thus that real happiness was to be won.

From this story was derived the first lesson in the earliest book of Christian instruction that has come down to us, the lesson on the two ways—the way of Life and the way of Death : a lesson that was much made use of by some of the earliest Christian writers. When one observes how many have gone far on the downward way without knowing it ; how often they are misled by the recuperative powers of nature, finding that they can do wrong and pay but slight penalty, ignorant what long accounts nature keeps, and how unfailingly she exacts at a distant time the penalty of forgotten sins, one is tempted to wish that a young man should be called on, like the Hercules of story, to make a formal choice between the rival claimants of his allegiance, and could hear the pleadings on both sides ; should learn from the one what inducements she had to offer, and should hear from the other side what her wages really are, and what the gift of God to those who choose the upward path. But such a wish is suggested by a false idea, like that of the rich man who imagined that his brethren would repent, if only one came to them who had risen from the dead, and who was told : " They have Moses and the prophets, let them hear them." Solicitous as we are that those young men in whom, during their residence here, we have learned to feel a strong interest, shall in their maturity be men of whom their university shall be proud, instead of leaving us cause for mourning over wasted powers, yet if they make a wrong choice they cannot complain that it was because they had not been sufficiently warned. Remember that every time that on the one side temptation entices you, and that on the other your conscience protests against it, then you hear a voice calling on you to make the gravest of all decisions : " Choose you this day whom you will serve." God grant each of you grace to answer : " As for me, I will serve the Lord."

SERMON III

RIGHTEOUS HATRED

"Ye that love the Lord, hate evil."—PSALM xcvii. 10.

THE precept of St Paul, "Be ye angry and sin not," has sometimes caused a little perplexity to a youthful reader, who, having been often scolded for getting into a passion, finds it hard to understand that indulging in anger can ever be anything but sinful. And the text I have read may too suggest the question, Is it possible that anger and hatred should be inculcated under a Gospel which ever breathes mercy, forgiveness, and loving kindness? Yet if we take note of the discipline by which we are trained to walk in the right course, we cannot help seeing that fear as well as love has its share in our instruction. God's law has its rewards for those who obey it, but also its penalties for those who transgress it; and God uses our fellowmen as His instruments both for bestowing happiness and in inflicting punishment. Need I say how our first happiness comes to us from love bestowed on us by others without any desert of ours; how continually our happiness is maintained by good offices rendered by our fellows—nay, how almost impossible it would be to sustain life itself, if all around us, even though abstaining from actively injuring us, simply agreed in leaving us to ourselves, and allowed us nothing save what by our unassisted exertions we could manage to procure for ourselves. Yet if our only experience of our fellowmen was the receiving benefits from them, what a training we should have got in selfish rapacity, always receiving, never giving, taking without gratitude what we should be accustomed to look on as our right, and regardless of any privation inflicted on others, if it might seem to contribute to our comfort. Happily the course of nature is not so constituted. Just as surely as a child learns that if he puts his finger into a flame it will be burned, so experience teaches him that if he insists on having his own will obeyed, without any attention to the claims or wishes of others, he will awake their resentment, and in a sorrowful lesson be made to feel the consequences of it. Reason is slow to operate, and the lesson needful for us would be learned too late, if it could not be taught us until a calculation had been made both by ourselves and by those on whose rights we were disposed to encroach, which of us had the best right to the things we were attempting to seize. But just as when we attempt to violate what we call the laws of nature quick punishment teaches us immediately how wrong we have been, so if we injure the person or property of others, their anger flames forth, and makes us suffer penalty for our misdoing, a penalty the justice of which is acknowledged by all around us. In short, injury to our neighbour is forbidden by a penal statute, the execution of which is in the first instance entrusted to the sufferer; and that divine gift of compassion which makes the infliction of pain repugnant to us, and thus would stand in the way of the criminal meeting his deserts, is kept in check by the equally divinely implanted feeling of indignation against wrong, which makes the infliction of retaliatory suffering both tolerable to ourselves, approved by disinterested onlookers, and even felt to be just by the criminal himself. If the expression of anger against ill usage can be stopped, power is in danger of degenerating into tyranny. It is often so in the case of a despotic monarch; it is sometimes so in the case of a school bully, who happens to be so much stronger than any of his schoolfellows that his commands must be obeyed without disputing— nay, even an amiable father of a family is in danger of becoming a tyrant if he is held in such respect by wife and children that they do not venture to remonstrate when he acts unreasonably.

But it is not by the actual infliction of penalties that the world is kept in moral order; it is rather by the public opinion generated by the knowledge that penalties are due and are likely to be inflicted. Our Lord rebuked the Pharisees because they loved the praise of men more than the praise of God. Now is it in itself a wrong thing to care for the praise of men? If this question were translated out of Scriptural language into the language of ordinary life, it would run: Would you call a man a good man if he cared nothing for the loss of his character? On the contrary, the esteem in which a man is held by others does so much to determine the amount of power and influence he can exercise that, provided that esteem has not been dishonourably won—not by a substitution of pretence for honest reality, not by puffing or self-advertisement—it is a valuable possession which a man would deserve to be scorned as a spendthrift if he threw lightly away. It is not the best people who have no regard for their character—nay, rather, it is those who have already sunk so low in the estimation of their fellows that the small shred of good repute that remains seems to them hardly worth the labour of preserving. How highly the praise of man is valued may be judged by the intensity of the strain that is experienced when it is felt that man's praise cannot be kept without losing the praise of God. Happily the world is so constituted that thinking men are convinced that God's commandments are not grievous—nay, rather that obedience to them is the surest way to happiness in this life, even for the man himself, as it undoubtedly is for the happiness of others. It follows that as a general rule, the conduct which men honour with their approbation, and which wins their esteem, is the conduct enjoined by God's law. But from time to time cases arise when it becomes our duty to say, We must obey God rather than man ; and how severe the conflict is then may be judged from the greatness of the multitude who fail in it. How rare is the courage to do what it is known will bring contempt and ridicule, even hatred, from all around.

Yet this law of opinion which is a tyrant to the weak, is a coward before those who defy it. When it is seen that refusal to obey is not prompted by perversity, or by a desire to win notoriety through singularity, but by honest belief in the real unlawfulness of what is demanded, then often public opinion wheels round and honours those whom it had held up to scorn.   There is no more striking example of this than what we find in the New Testament of the history of the first preachers of Christianity.   Their work was decidedly condemned by public opinion, both Jew and Gentile.   " Those that turned the world upside down " was one of the mildest names bestowed on them.   Our Lord had warned them what was before them, when He directed them to count themselves blessed when men should hate them and separate themselves from their company, and reproach them and cast out their name as evil, for the Son of Man's sake.   And such was their actual experience as described by the apostle : " Being reviled, we bless ; being persecuted, we suffer it ; being defamed, we intreat : we are made as the filth of the world, and are the off-scouring of all things to this day."   And yet concerning those who suffered shame for the name of Jesus, we may ask, Where is the shame now ?   If the praise of men were the thing that men ought to seek after, who have done it so successfully as these twelve men who now, some two thousand years after their death, are held in honour all over the civilised world ?

The honour bestowed on those who have successfully braved public opinion and brought it round to agreement with themselves, is sufficient evidence how severely the strain of such opposition is felt by ordinary people.   Happily, it is only occasionally that the duty devolves on any one of defying public opinion ; but we are, every one, engaged in the business of forming public opinion.   Just as the mightiest ocean wave is but the aggregate of some millions of tiny drops of water, so the practically irresistible judgment of society is no more than the aggregate of the judgments of a multitude of individuals, none of whom, as a general rule, is more deserving of consideration than ourselves. The judgment which one expresses in his own little circle, and with which his hearers agree, when repeated by each of them, wins a multitude of new adherents, and becomes the judgment of the community. So the responsibility lies on all of us to take heed that we judge right judgments.

But it is not by arguments convincing the cold reason of those who listen to them that our opinion spreads; for man is very far from being a being moved to a decision by reason only. What passes rapidly from one to another is sympathetic emotion. I have spoken already of the feeling of resentment against injury, a feeling which no doubt is felt most strongly by the sufferer. But when there has been wrong and injustice, the bystanders likewise feel indignation, and the criminal himself is constrained by conscience to self-condemnation. A fictitious story will suffice to stir this feeling of indignation. You remember how, when Nathan told David the fictitious story of the rich man, who spared to take of his own flocks or herds to dress for the guest who came to him, but seized on his poor neighbour's lamb, which had lain in his bosom, and been to him as a daughter, the King's indignation burst out, and he declared that the man who had done this thing should surely die. It has often been found dangerous to act in a play the part of a villain before a rude audience accustomed to put no restraint on the expression of its feelings, and capable of proceeding to personal violence against one who shocks their moral judgments. It is this explosion of emotion which makes public opinion really formidable. When no moral judgments are shocked, we feel ourselves quite free to disregard the opinions of others. For example, a moneyed man making an investment would, of course, give full consideration to the fact that what he was thinking of was regarded as imprudent by some competent judges ; but if he had more confidence in his own opinion, he would not hesitate to act in opposition to theirs, and he would not imagine that they had any right to be angry with him for so doing. It is quite otherwise if we discover a man to be a liar or a coward ; even though we are not in the least personally affected by his mis-conduct, he does not escape our scorn. It is by the dread of social stigma that the high standard of female purity which prevails among us is kept up ; and though, as regards the other sex, the standard enforced by public opinion is far lower, yet we have not been without examples in recent years that flagrant violations of this part of the moral law will make right-thinking men unwilling to act with the offender in other business. But in order to show what force the opinion of others exercises on us, I need not take extreme cases of social ostracism. In the presence of a single man of high character, and still more in that of a good woman, a profane jeer, an obscene jest, a cynical confession of conduct which men agree in counting dishonourable, dies on the lips of him who might be inclined to make it, through his knowledge of the disgust such language would inspire. It is this force of opinion which keeps

the world in order. What prevents a soldier from
running away is not the fear that his general might
order him to be shot; it is fear of being scorned by
his comrades, and still more, his own sympathy with
their feeling, which makes him incapable of conduct
for which he would scorn himself.

Yet powerful as is this force of opinion, I have
already had occasion to say how weak it is when
defied. It is often, thank God, changed for the
better; it has been so changed even during the century which is approaching its end—changed, for
instance, as to duelling, as to the habit of hard drink-
ing, as to the use of profane or indecent language.
But it can also be changed for the worse, and more
easily. I do not know why an insolvent debtor should
consider that he rises in the moral scale by becoming
a repudiator; but the idea is not uncommon, and in
matters of morality especially, it sometimes happens
that men who fail to fulfil their obligations, hope to
get on good terms with their own consciences and
those of others by finding out that it had been a mistake all along to imagine that they were bound by
them. Of course the claim meets sympathy from
persons who had also been worsted in a conflict
between duty and inclination; and there are others,
too, for whom a paradox has a strong attraction, with
whom any attempt to overthrow a received opinion
finds a favourable reception.

In former days a claim was easily admitted on
behalf of men of high rank that they were too great
to be fettered by the restrictions to which the vulgar
herd must submit; but, partly owing to the growth of
democratic ideas, and partly to good example set in

C

high quarters, that claim is not heard of now, and there is no rank in which vice can now be unblushingly avowed, as it could a century or two ago. But we do sometimes hear the same claim made on behalf of men of genius, that they are too great to be bound by ordinary laws, and that we ought to allow ourselves to be bribed to excuse their moral delinquencies in consideration of the pleasure their works give us; and if these works are demoralising and corrupting, we are told that art is one thing and morality another; and that if the art be good we are to admire without troubling ourselves about the morality. But though in the region of abstract ideas art and morality are different, yet when we have to deal with concrete facts we cannot, in judging of anything, take count only of one of its attributes, disregarding the others. An ancient philosopher justified the poetical garb in which he clothed his lessons by the practice of physicians who, to induce a child to swallow the bitter healing draught, smear the edges of the cup with honey. But suppose the same artifice were used to disguise a poisonous mixture, would it avail to say confectionery and medicine are different arts; considered from a medical point of view, no doubt, the draught is noxious; but, as it is pleasant to the taste, it may be taken?

Diversity of judgment sometimes arises from opposite defects in the organs of taste. Many a pious person, for example, has used with great enjoyment a hymn which disgusts one whose sense of beauty has been more cultivated, by its mixture of metaphors and the poverty of its language. But, on the other hand, just as persons who have no sense of smell can be contented in a malodorous atmosphere, so there are people who, however moral their own actions may be, seem to have no moral sense, and feel no disgust at what is foul and base if it does not injuriously affect themselves.   Such persons cannot understand how what they admire for its beauty should be absolutely repulsive to others.   If it is a loss to a man to be without an ear for music, without any sense of the harmony of deftly collocated words, without power of appreciating the beauty of a fine painting, it is a far greater loss to be without the power of loving moral beauty and hating moral ugliness ; and it is no less than a national calamity if this defect spreads to the community.   There is no greater injury done to society than by those who teach men to call evil good and good evil.   The Psalmist gives the last touch to his picture of the wicked man who has no fear of God before his eyes by adding : " Neither doth he abhor anything that is evil."

I must not omit to mention, in conclusion, one cause which tends to weaken those feelings which operate in making us recoil from vice, and visit those who are guilty of it with our disapprobation—I mean our sense of compassion.   It is natural to us all to indulge our inclinations without thinking much about right and wrong as long as wrong-doing is visited with no penalty.   It is part of the goodness of God that we are checked by the sting of pain when we do what is injurious to body or soul.   If the penalty is one to be inflicted by our fellowmen, they would be checked by their feeling of pity if that feeling were not opposed by their feeling of righteous indignation against wrong.   The latter feeling is not too strong in any of us, and anything that tends to weaken it is an injury to society. Yet men are not wholly bad; the greatest villain has some redeeming points; and one who fixes his attention solely on these cannot help feeling for suffering endured by one in some respects so estimable. It may be the deserved result of his wrong-doing; but we are tempted to ask: Is not the law too severe? especially when we are called on to notice that many escape its penalties who are not really more to be liked than those who suffer from them. This is a favourite topic with some popular modern works of fiction which, as our late Viceroy[1] expressed it, occupy themselves much in exciting sympathy for the sorrows of misbelieving men and misbehaving women. But pity would be misleading if it tended to obliterate in our minds the distinction between right and wrong, and through its compassionate estimate of vice taught us first to endure, then pity, then embrace. In things that affect ourselves, however mercifully we may be disposed, there are penalties that we cannot remit. If we find that a man has been in the habit of telling us lies, we can't help being slow to believe his statements again. If one whom we have trusted has robbed us, we may mercifully decline to prosecute, but we do not put more of our money into his power; nor would it be friendly if we allowed others to do so. And however lenient our judgment of his case, we have no inclination to say: After all, though lying and stealing are condemned by the conventions of society, they do not really so much matter, and he is a very good fellow notwithstanding. And are we to confine severity of

---

[1] Lord Houghton, now Earl of Crewe.

judgment to cases in which ourselves have been sufferers? If a man shows himself a coward, are we to respect him? If through inability to deny his appetites any gratification he ruins himself, can we say he does not deserve his fate? What if in his self-indulgence he ruins not only himself but his wife and family—nay, what if in his licence he brings shame and unhappiness into the house of another, do we not well to be angry? The feelings that make us recoil from wickedness and loathe it, are nothing to be ashamed of. They are the very salt of the life of the world. "Ye then that love the Lord, hate evil," but most of all hate it in yourselves. Hate it not only in the form which you condemn, and which may have no attraction for you; but in other forms which you may be more inclined to. Give no cause that it should be said of you: "Thou that judgest another, judgest thou not thyself?"

SERMON IV

THE WORTH OF THE ONE TALENT

"But he that had received the one talent went and digged in the earth, and hid his lord's money."—MATT. xxv. 18.

THE fact that the day happens to be Sunday, when the Church commemorates the apostles St Simon and St Jude, gives to that festival more prominence than it has in ordinary years. It is a natural thought, on hearing the mention of their names, that one should ask oneself why we should commemorate men of whom we know so little. We have, indeed, a short epistle bearing the name of Jude, and one saying of that apostle is recorded by St John; but nothing else that he said or did is related either in the Gospels or in the Acts; and of Simon we find in those books nothing recorded at all.

Yet though we have no detailed information as to the life of these men, we know that they were entrusted with an important work, and we have no reason to doubt that they did it faithfully and well. Their names are included in the list of those Twelve whom our Lord Himself chose to be His companions, and whom He left to be rulers over the Church which He founded. All through the early chapters of the Acts, we find "the Twelve" presiding over the Church and directing its affairs. And surely never was there a society whose affairs were conducted with such success. Their prospects at the beginning, to an outsider, would have seemed hopeless. Their Founder had been put to a shameful death, and the baselessness of His pretensions had, as it was thought, been thoroughly exposed. The hand of authority had been heavy on His surviving disciples, and stripes and imprisonment were their portion when they still persisted in asserting their Master's Messiahship. Yet the new faith spread with marvellous rapidity. "Ye have filled Jerusalem with your teaching" was the high priest's complaint ; and soon the new religion passed far outside Jerusalem. We do not know the exact date of St Paul's conversion, but some very good chronologers have placed it so early as within a year of the Ascension ; and you know from the story that at that time there were Christians outside the Holy Land, in the Syrian city of Damascus, in sufficient number to demand the attention of the rulers. Not very long after, another Syrian city, Antioch, is found full of Christian life, and has become the centre of the first missionary organisation. In distant lands the Christian society established itself ; but everywhere the authority of the Twelve was recognised. In remote Galatia Paul's authority was disputed because he was not of the number, and was imagined to be at variance with them. Thus, though the spread of Christianity owed much (perhaps owed most) to the exertions of preachers not numbered in the Twelve, to the deacons, Stephen and Philip, in the earliest stages, and to the new apostles, Paul and Barnabas, at a later time, yet the Twelve held the principal place

in the government of the Church; and we are told
that, when persecution scattered the other disciples
away from Jerusalem, the Twelve remained behind.
Now, of the actual work of the Twelve we are told no
particulars, except in the case of Peter and John, and
perhaps I should add of James, if I am wrong in
thinking that the James in question was not one of
the original Twelve. But we hear of Peter and
John going away on missionary tours, so that it
follows that much of the work of guiding and
ruling the Church of Jerusalem, and through it the
whole Christian community, must have been done
by those obscure members of the Twelve concerning whose life we are told nothing. Of such men
St Simon and St Jude may be regarded as typical
representatives. I use, then, the opportunity to
speak of the value, in God's sight, of the commonplace work done by such persons as these, of whom
the bulk of every community must consist; who do
not stand out above the rest either by their station or
for their ability; who can have little hope that their
names will be venerated by posterity in connection
with any signal service which they might have had
the happiness to render; and who, having been only
called to serve their own generation, through the will
of God, in the performance of routine duties are, after
their death, soon forgotten by men, but are not forgotten by Him who, in the great day, may bestow on
them the high and sufficient commendation He gave
to one of old, " She hath done what she could." I feel it
to be a far more practical subject to speak of the
honour that is due to those who employ one talent
faithfully than to call to mind the glory that has been

won by those who have nobly made use of ten. To the former class must belong the majority even of such a congregation as this. Young men may have sanguine dreams that they will one day stand high above their fellows, but usually their ambitious hopes are disappointed ; and there are many who very early find that such hopes are not for them.

And it occurs to me now to remind you how we lately celebrated the 300th year of this University ; yet, if you were asked to name the persons through whom it grew from small beginnings to the place among learned societies that it now occupies, you might be puzzled to answer. It would be easy to name many of our graduates of whom we are justly proud ; but these are, almost all, men who went out from us, of whom we boast only because they received their education here, but of those who gave them that education we keep little memory. I could name those who, in my early days, according to my judgment, did most service in raising the standard of our education and directing our affairs, but to the generation which has grown to manhood since their death they are but mere names, and in the next generation their very names are likely to be forgotten.

After all, it is by the common soldiers that every battle must be won. Far be it from me to disparage the merit of the few or the one who may be in command, without whose wise direction all the force might spend its strength to no profit, and from sympathy with whose inspiriting example every member has derived the energy which has multiplied his powers ; but the fact remains that one man, or a few men, can, by themselves, do little, and the best general is he who can weld an army into a harmonious whole, making his captains into a band of brothers, and every common soldier as lion-hearted as himself. And so of the Church. It is, as the apostle teaches, an organised body, consisting of many members, varying much both in their powers and in the functions which they have to discharge, but even those members which seem to be more feeble are necessary. The more honourable, as the apostle teaches, have no reason to despise those who are less so. The eye cannot say to the hand, I have no need of thee ; nor, again, the head to the feet, I have no need of you. Neither, again, have the less honoured members cause to despise their position because the work given to them to do is not accounted so noble as that fulfilled by others. " If the foot shall say, Because I am not the hand I am not of the body, is it therefore not of the body? If all were one member where were the body ? " All that a loyal soldier has to care for is the victory of the army to which he belongs. Where he himself shall be placed, and how much he shall contribute to the victory, is for the general to arrange and not for him. All his part is to take care that his commander shall not be disappointed in expecting that, wherever he may be posted, he will do his duty. And so we pray to that God by whose Spirit the whole body of the Church is sanctified and governed, for all estates of men in His holy Church, that every member of the same in his vocation and ministry may truly and godly serve Him.

In the verse I read for my text a temptation is glanced at to which those to whom only one talent has been given are exposed—namely, to think their work not worth doing. In the parable we are told that those to whom five talents or ten talents had been entrusted, traded with them and made profit on them. It was the man of one talent who counted the probable gain too small to compensate the risk, and who thought his safest course was to bury his talent in the earth. And, naturally, this is a temptation which does not much beset those endowed with larger gifts ; for there is a great pleasure in doing what we can feel we are doing well, to say nothing of the immediate reward to be gained in the credit that follows successful performance of work. And yet it has often occurred to me to doubt whether even the well-endowed always escape the sin of burying talents unfruitfully. It may happen that the man to whom ten talents had been given makes a profit of five, and gains reputation among men by the largeness of his gain ; and yet it may be that, when his Master comes to reckon with him, he shall incur reproof because, yielding to the seduction of indolence, or the attractions of idle pleasure, he has buried five of his talents in the earth, and traded only with five.

But indolence and pleasure have attractions for the poorly gifted as well as for the richly endowed, and there is not for the former the countervailing attraction of the prospect of seeing good fruit of his labours. Yet the success of our work is to be judged, not by the estimate which other men put on it, still less by the estimate which we ourselves put on it, but by the judgment of the Master who has appointed our work; who is not an austere man, gathering where He has not strawed, but one who will require from us

no more than what the deposit committed to us, if
honestly used, ought to yield. To scorn our work
because the part we play seems to us a poor one,
is the same as if a chorus singer considered that
because he knew that his powers were not adequate
to the undertaking of a solo, therefore it was needless for him to take pains with the part committed
to him. If all judged so, where would be the
harmony?

Happily, we are so constituted that the fault of
underrating the importance of our efforts is not that
into which people are most apt to fall. I suppose,
on the contrary, it must often happen to us, in the
case of matters in which we ourselves take no interest,
to feel some kind of pitying contempt for the importance men attach to the exertions they make,
as it seems to our unsympathetic gaze, with little
advantage to anybody. To people who have no
pursuits of their own, the activity of others seems
a busy idleness as unmeaning as the motions of a
dance are apt to appear to those who cannot hear
the music; and so satirists who have no pursuit of
their own save to write cleverly of the follies of
others, have found it easy to mock at the cares of
men and the vanity of human affairs. We too often
see good grounds for such mockery, though sometimes pity is too great for laughter; I mean when
we are forcibly struck with the irony of the contrast
between expectation and probable result, on witnessing the sanguine efforts to gain fortune or fame by
achievements which we know to be either impossible
or beyond the powers of those who attempt them.
It is sometimes a pathetic sight when an old man,

who has done good work in earlier days, has persuaded himself that he will be able with the last efforts of a toilworn brain to bequeath to posterity some possession for ever which they shall value far beyond anything which he or any one else has previously produced.

But we need not confine our view to the case of the men who have failed, and draw a contrast between the actual result of their labour and the undue estimate they had themselves formed of its importance. May we not make the same remark in the case of many of those who not only supposed themselves to have succeeded, but who gained the applause of their own generation? How many volumes that made great reputation in their time now stand on the shelves of our great libraries unopened from one year to another, because the controversies which they were imagined to have determined have utterly lost their interest for the present generation, which can scarcely understand how men could have been so foolish as to fight about them! Even the works of many of those authors whose names we still quote with honour may be said to be dead as far as the knowledge of the present day is concerned, because, notwithstanding their celebrity, they are not read, except that in our days a certain artificial prolongation of their existence has been gained through the necessity imposed on students of giving some account of them at examinations.

What inference are we to draw from the fact that men in general are far more apt to put too high than too low an estimate on the importance of the work they do? Is it that none of our work is really worth the pains we bestow on it? Surely we ought to draw just the opposite inference from the fact that the error against which our Maker seems most anxious to guard us, is that of under-valuing the importance of our work, and so being tempted to bury our talent. The true inference, rather, is that those differences of small and great importance, which seem to us so wide, may in our Lord's sight be far less than in our thinking, or may even be reversed. He who deemed the widow's mite a greater gift than all that the rich men had poured into the treasury, may pronounce the honest fulfilment of a humble task a greater service for Him than pretentious labours on which men have bestowed honour. Differences of height which seem considerable when looked at from below, shrink into insignificance when all are looked at from a much greater height above. A good man of the last century asked whether, if God sent two angels into the world, and commissioned one to sweep a crossing and the other to rule a kingdom, we could imagine the latter triumphing over his fellow because the duty entrusted to him was so much more dignified.

If mistakes are sometimes made in estimating how much particular individuals have contributed to the progress of humanity, the fact remains that the human race does progress in knowledge, in power, in stored-up capital ; what that progress owes to the contribution of some remarkable individuals is the thing that most arrests our attention. But when we examine, we find that the work done has really been effected by the accumulation of the silent efforts of a multitude of undistinguished units. The greatest test of the merit of an individual is what impulse he is able to give to others. The spirit of one man passes by a sympathetic contagion into the hearts of those who come within the sphere of his influence, just as a few drops of leaven introduced in a mass rapidly spread their influence through the whole mass, each new particle affected by it becoming a new centre of diffusion until the entire is leavened.

Thus in the great revolutionary war, the spirit of a few brave men rapidly became universal through the English navy, and though the first great victory of 1st June was won, notwithstanding that some captains took care to keep their ships out of harm's way, such backwardness soon became a thing unheard of. No more was heard of the idea that it was unsafe to make an attack at night, because then cowardice could escape undetected ; and an admiral could enter at nightfall into an unknown haven to attack a superior force in the full certainty that every ship would follow, and that duty would be done as honestly in the dark as in the light.

If we speak of leaven it must be owned by all, that never in the world's history was such vivifying influence communicated to a mass as when our blessed Lord came upon the earth. If we neither knew what He was, nor had any report of what He did or said, still history would bear witness to the power of His influence, and the rapidity with which it spread. Scarcely had the efforts of those who feared or hated Him attained, as it seemed, the highest success, when those who had been touched by His spirit had become centres of its diffusion, and were rapidly spreading His doctrine, and multiplying the preachers of it first through Judea, soon through the whole

Roman world. It needed not that any of these disciples should be a man of transcendent ability; it sufficed that he should have companied with Jesus. Imagine one of those less prominent apostles of whom I spoke at the beginning. Let him have been a commonplace man of very ordinary ability, and yet in the city where he dwelt what influence could be compared to his? What Church orator could speak with such persuasive influence as he who could repeat in simple words the lessons he had learned from his Lord, and who could show in the whole tenor of his life that he had made those lessons his own?

Was it only in the first century that such men could be found? Is it not true that Jesus lives: that it is possible still to hold intercourse with Him— possible for any of you to be such that men may take knowledge of you, that you have been with Jesus? It matters not that you are conscious that you have little power and small influence. It is not you who can effect anything, but the spirit which dwells in you, and which, if you do not quench it, will through you inspire others, and gain other agents to work for Him. What more feeble than a drop of water? what more powerful than the many drops collected into a mighty wave? There is no force so effective in the affairs of men as the public opinion of a society. Yet that is but the aggregate of the opinions of a multitude of individuals. It can easily be affected; the moral tone of a whole nation may be depressed by a few who think and talk lightly of sin; it can be sustained by even insignificant persons who resolutely refuse to call evil good and good evil.

Many a man to whom it would not occur to cry: "How shall I do this great wickedness and sin against God?" will yet dread to do a shameful thing by which he would lose the respect of his wife or his sister or his daughter. It needs not that one should be high or great to exercise an influence which will bear fruit in this world after his own life has closed. Many a one there has been whom there have been none to praise, few to love, or even to know when she had ceased to be, yet whose departure left, in the hearts of the few who knew and loved, an irreparable blank, when that first dark day of nothingness left behind only a fragrant memory of gracious words, kindly deeds, sorrows consoled, dissensions appeased, suffering patiently and cheerfully borne. Let no one dare to think his work too humble to need to be done faithfully, but let each do with all his might that work, great or small, which God has put it in his hand to find to do; for many there be whose work in men's eyes has been of poor account, who, in the day when all secrets shall be disclosed, shall shine like the Sun in the kingdom of their Father.

SERMON V

DO WE LOVE OUR LORD?

"Jesus saith to Simon Peter, Simon, son of Jonas, lovest thou Me more than these?"—JOHN xxi. 15.

WHERE love is perfect and acknowledged this question, "Do you love me?" is not put; for it is felt it can be taken for granted. Nay, protestations of love, if excessive, raise a doubt of the sincerity of the affection which cannot be believed in by its object without such protestations. The question, "Do you love me?" may be put for one or another of two reasons. It may be put in the confident hope that it can be answered affirmatively, and with the expectation that the profession will give strength to the feelings which it acknowledges, and will warrant a demand that the love which is professed shall show itself in action. But the question may also be put in reproach, "*Do* you love me?" if the love that has been professed has not shown itself in action—nay, rather, if the conduct has been such as to give reasonable cause for doubt whether the affection once professed has ever existed, or at anyrate whether it exists now.

In Peter's case he had good reason for thinking that the question might well have been put in re-

proach.   How could he remember without shame that
he who had once protested that he would go with his
Lord to prison or to death—that if he should die
with Him, he would not deny Him—had yet failed
in the hour of trial, and had protested with
an oath that he did not know his Master.
No wonder that he should be grieved at the
thrice repeated question which seemed to indicate
that no confidence was felt in professions which
had already been proved to be worthless.   To
me it is rather wonderful that it was only on the
third putting of the question that Peter was grieved ;
for the very first question might well have suggested
an abashed recollection of the past, and a timorous
doubt whether any value could now be attached to
his protestations.   It seems to me not impossible,
since we are told that before this interview our Lord
had appeared to Simon, that he might have already
made confession of sin and have obtained his Master's
assurance of forgiveness.   At all events, Peter believed
that he was speaking to One who knew what was in
man.   If he made professions to any one else his
sincerity might be doubted ; but Jesus would know
that his words expressed the real thoughts of his
heart.

I will not say that there was absolutely nothing of
reproach in the question, "Lovest thou Me more than
these ? "   The last three words may be understood in
different ways, but, understood in one way, they touch
the point of Peter's frailty.   He could confidently say
that he loved his Master.   We cannot doubt that he
sincerely did love Him, even at the moment he
denied Him.   But the event showed that at this time

he loved other things more—that he loved his own safety more. He had not known that this was so when he spoke the brave words, "I will go with Thee to prison or to death." He had been ready to fight for his Master, and doubtless had faith to believe that in His strength he must be victorious. But that was not what he was asked to do. His Master had refused to allow him to fight for Him, and now the question was, would he suffer with Him—suffer, as it would seem, unavailingly. In the end he was able to show that he loved his Master, so as not to shrink from suffering or shame for His sake. But just then the very blow he had struck so unavailingly robbed his heart of courage, through the feeling that he would be himself marked out for punishment for an act which his Master disowned.

But, however, it was mainly *not* in reproach that our Lord's question was put. It was with the other purpose I have described—namely, with the intention that, by forcing the apostle to acknowledge, and thus become fully conscious of the affection which he really felt, his mind might be prepared to give the proof of love which He was about to demand. No wonder that Peter could only regard the question as a reproach! For it could scarcely occur to him that his risen Lord could need any service that he could do for Him.

I do not think there is any more striking coincidence between the reports of the language of Jesus given by different evangelists than the coincidence—not indeed in words but in thought—between our Lord's words recorded by St Matthew, "Inasmuch as ye did it unto the least of these My brethren ye did it unto Me?" and these words reported by St John, "Do you

love Me? If so, how shall you show your love?"
"Feed my sheep." In other words, services rendered
to Christ's people are acknowledged by Him as done
to Himself, and are regarded as the best way in which
a man can show his love to Him.

"Feed My sheep." This phrase, "My sheep," could
not but bring to Peter's mind our Lord's discourse
which St John has recorded in chapter x., in
which that phrase so often occurs. "I know My
sheep and am known of Mine": "I lay down My
life for the sheep," "My sheep hear My voice, and I
know them, and they follow Me." On account of the
difference in style between the discourses of our Lord,
as recorded by St John and by the other three
Evangelists, a question has been raised as to whether
St John's report is trustworthy; so I may here say,
in passing, with regard to the discourse in John x.,
that we have the best possible evidence, through coin-
cidences with other New Testament writings, either
that they were acquainted with St John's Gospel, and
accepted it as trustworthy, or else that St John has
reported a real discourse of our Lord with which these
other writers had an independent acquaintance; and
it is not surprising to find that the most striking
coincidence is with the Epistle of Peter himself.

You will observe that in those passages of St John,
which speak of the shepherding of Christ's flock, there
is a twofold conception—of our Lord Himself as the
Chief Shepherd, which is so fully developed in chapter
x., and that which we find in our text of subordinate
shepherds employed under His superintendence to feed
and tend the portion of the flock committed to them.
Both these conceptions we find reproduced in St

Peter's Epistle, where he passes on to the elders who then ruled the Church, the exhortation which he had himself received from his Master. He says, "Feed the flock of God which is among you, taking the oversight thereof not by constraint, but willingly—not as lords over God's heritage, but being examples to the flock. And when the 'Chief Shepherd' shall appear, ye shall receive a crown of glory that fadeth not away." You will find the same exhortation to feed the flock in St Paul's address to the elders of Ephesus recorded in Acts xx.; and the same recognition of our Lord's own office as Chief Shepherd in the title given him in the Epistle to the Hebrews, "That great Shepherd of the sheep."

When Peter was first called to be an apostle, our Lord's words to him were "From henceforth thou shalt catch men." And the work in which by these words his success was predicted would seem to be only that of bringing new disciples into the fold. This was, of necessity, the first thing to be done, but it was only the beginning. The new disciples would need instruction and practical guidance, and our Lord foresaw and provided for this need when His own presence should be removed. The double work which the Christian pastor has to do is indicated by the use of two different Greek words in the commission to Peter; and though the distinction was lost sight of in the Authorised Version, it has been preserved in the Revised Version, which represents our Lord as saying, "Feed My sheep," and, "Tend My sheep"; the one, as I take it, referring to the work of instruction, the other to that of guidance—to the task of warning against temptation, of striving to keep the

flock from turning into evil ways, and of leading them
into the pastures where their souls will be fed.

The text contains a twofold lesson—one for the
members of the flock, the other for him who takes
on himself the office of their pastor. The lesson for
the flock is not to despise the guidance which Christ
has provided for them, nor imagine that they can
safely dispense with what He has judged necessary.
Jude, in his Epistle, draws a picture of the fall of
those who, in the Authorised Version, are described
as *feeding* themselves without fear—but as it ought
rather to be rendered, who shepherd themselves without fear ; that is to say, who are not afraid to be
their own shepherds, who despise dominions, and
speak evil of dignities, who separate themselves, and
walk after their own lusts.

On the other hand, for him who would take on him
the office of a pastor, the question is suggested, Why
do you undertake the office ? Is it from love of Christ,
and from a sense of the obligation to show your
gratitude for what He has done for you, in the way
which He has commanded—namely, by services to His
sheep? If any are actuated by lower motives they
have reason to fear that they lie under the woe which,
through the mouth of Ezekiel, God denounced against
the shepherds who feed themselves and not the flock ;
who allow the flocks to wander through the mountains,
and on every high hill, and to be scattered on the face
of the earth, while none searcheth or looketh after
them. However, if we would learn all the practical
lessons that are taught by the text, we must not limit
our view to that particular proof of love which our
Lord demanded of Peter, contenting ourselves merely

with enquiring how proof of the same kind can be given in our day. For God bestows manifold diversity of gifts, and every gift of His can be employed in His service. Different servants of His may love Him equally, but be called on to show their love in different ways. The works done are diverse, but the animating principle of all is the same, and the one great question for us is whether or not that principle reigns in our own hearts. How should we reply if the question addressed to Peter were put to us—Do we love our Lord?

That it should be possible to put to us that question now, nearly two thousand years after the death of Jesus of Nazareth, at once places Him on a different pedestal from any other who trod this earth, however great he may have been. For the great men of old we may feel admiration when their story is told us. If they have done services to the world, of which we ourselves reap some portion of the benefit, we may feel gratitude to them; or perhaps it would be more accurate to say that we would be not un-willing to acknowledge that they deserved that we ought to be grateful to them; but does such admira-tion or gratitude deserve to be honoured with the name of love?

Love begets love. As the apostle said of our love to God, we love Him because He first loved us. And though it would of course be untrue to say that love never arises except in answer to love, for it is in the nature of things necessary that one of the two parties should make the beginning, yet the best part of human love is that which grows in answer to love; for love, if not responded to, is chilled and languishes, and only by a struggle can be kept alive; but when heart answers to heart, the love of each is warmed and expanded by the love of the other.

Gratitude can never grow into love except through recognition of the good-will of him from whom the benefit is derived. Sometimes it happens that acts committed with hostile intention, in the result confer benefit rather than injury. In that case we accept the benefit, but we feel neither gratitude nor love. Even in the absence of evil intention, if there is no evidence of real wish to do us good, our gratitude does not arise. A machine may be extremely useful to us; we may value it highly, and would be exceedingly sorry to be deprived of it, yet it would be an abuse of the word love to employ that word to express our feelings towards it. And to take perhaps the strongest case of benefits conferred upon us without personal good-will, if we were in the enjoyment of an endowment founded by a pious benefactor a century ago, who, though he could have had no knowledge of us personally, intended to benefit the class to which we belonged, we should feel his memory well deserving of honour; possibly everything we might learn of his life might command our admiration, yet our gratitude for the advantage we derived from his pious forethought would scarce deserve to be called love. If we can use that word in respect of Jesus, it is because we count Him as no dead benefactor; not a good man who lived a blameless and useful life some centuries ago, not a wise teacher who benefited his own generation by words which had an abiding influence on the generations that came after, and by which ourselves have profited; it is because of our firm conviction that Jesus lives and loves us now, that it is possible for us to feel that answer of heart to heart to which we give the name of love.

It needs no lengthened proof that it is possible to love Jesus. Love to Him has for century after century been the animating principle of many thousands of the purest and noblest lives, and has been the motive spring of all their best actions ; men have been ready, for the sake of that love, to sacrifice all else that ordinary men count worth having. I doubt not that there are many here who can tell, not by the report of others, but from their own experience, what force that principle possesses. And I suppose all here will acknowledge that Jesus deserves to be loved, and that we ought to love Him. Yet the question re- mains—Do we ? What answer could we make if our Lord put to us His question to Peter : "Lovest thou Me ?"

John Newton, the well-known evangelical leader of a century ago, discussed that question with his friend, the poet Cowper ; and they have each given their answers in verse, which Newton included in his collection of Olney Hymns. Cowper's answer— the beautiful hymn, "Hark, my soul, it is the Lord !"—still deservedly keeps its place in almost all collections of sacred poetry. I cannot say I like so well Newton's own contribution, which begins :—

> "'Tis a point I long to know :
>   Oft it causes anxious thought :
>   Do I love the Lord or no ?
>   Am I His or am I not ?"

Probably he would have rejected the criticism ; but

his way of putting the question suggests to me the
idea that he was less anxious to know whether he
loved the Lord than whether the Lord loved him ;
and that he tried to answer that question by examining into the state of his own feelings. " Perfect love
casteth out fear " ; and conversely an alloy of fear
sadly debases the sincerity of love. If we tried the
experiment on any children of threatening to punish
them severely if they did not love us, we might easily
obtain professions of love, but I should doubt the
ardour of their affection. I believe that examination
into the state of our feelings is a very deceptive form
of self-examination, and, according to the difference
in men's temperaments, would in some cases produce
undue self-confidence, in others unreasonable despondency. Love thrives best when it can be taken
for granted, when it occurs to neither party to ask
whether or not he loves the other. Cross-examining
ourselves as to the state of our emotions has very
much the same effect as when children dig up their
seeds in order to find whether they are growing—the
effect, namely, of killing the growth which is investi-
gated. The best proof that seeds are sprouting is to
see something springing from them.

We must not mistake for moral faults what really
results from intellectual differences, and sometimes
from variations in the state of our bodies. When, for
example, the pious authoress of a well-known hymn
describes her heart as faithless, treacherous, cold, I
am persuaded that in the severity of her self-condemnation she did herself great injustice, merely
because sometimes she found herself quite incapable of the same liveliness of emotion which she

had experienced at other times. People also differ very much in their power of expressing their feelings in words. If we used their possession of this faculty as a measure of their sincerity, we should be bound to prefer a Regan or a Goneril to a Cordelia. And those who find a difficulty in expressing their feelings in spoken words are apt to find the same difficulty in making their thoughts assume those definite forms, of which words are the expression. Many a woman would be willing to make any sacrifice, suffer any pain, would give life itself for the sake of her husband or her children, who, if asked to shut herself up in her closet and meditate for half an hour on her husband's perfections, would find the time hang very heavy on her hands. If you wish to know how much original mental differences and the amount of mental cultivation have to say to such matters, you need only ask yourself whether you would be surprised if the most pious of ploughmen found himself unable to spend ten minutes in sacred meditations in which such a man as Canon Liddon could occupy himself for an hour or two. God is no respecter of persons, and the peasant is as acceptable to him as the scholar.

I should be sorry if any of you took up the idea that I was disparaging the advantage of religious meditation, or that I was teaching that the best way to love God was to do our secular duties and think no more about Him. All I am pointing out is the mistake of imagining that we do not belong to Christ because when we try to judge by examining into the state of our own emotions we do not find them as lively as they ought to be, and not as lively at some

times as at other times. The judgment likely to be
thus suggested is as Newton described it :—

> " If I love why am I thus?
>   Why this dull, this lifeless frame?
> Hardly, sure, can they be worse
>   Who have never heard His name."

But it is unquestionable that the power of loving
grows with our intellectual development, and with
our power of knowing and realising the facts which
justify love. No sensible parent would be much
distressed, or would set down his child as heartless,
because its feelings seemed cold, and it did not make
those gushing demonstrations of affection that some
exceptional children are able to do. Whether as
years go on the one would really love better than the
other may well be doubted, and a wise man would
be content not to judge before the time, but would
wait patiently until, with the growth of other powers,
the power of loving also expands. Possibly no one
fully knows what he has owed to his parents until
he has become a parent himself, and, having had
experience of that love which gives and asks not and
expects not return, he bethinks himself how much of
that self-sacrificing love had once been bestowed on
himself, and had been received as a matter of course
without stirring any gratitude. If then, you understand how increase of knowledge will bring increase
of love, you will perceive that if you have cause to
complain of the coldness of your love to Christ, the
remedy is not to scold yourself for not loving Him
better, but to try to know Christ better ; for the more
you know Him the more cause you will find for love
to Him.

And there is another way of stirring up our love to Him—namely, to work for Him. When our Lord asked that question of Peter, it was not to set him upon idle self-examination, but because He had a work to give him by which to show his love. It is a commonplace observation that the performance of acts of love does more to stir up love in him who does them than in him who is profited by them. The two things react on each other. Love prompts acts of love, and the performance of acts of love increases love. If, then, when you test by examining your feelings, you have any doubt whether you love Christ, act as if you did ; and the same Spirit who has given you grace to work for Him will also shed His love abroad in your hearts. We can well join in the prayer with which Newton concludes his hymn :—

> " Let me love Thee more and more
>   If I love at all, I pray
>   If I have not loved before,
>   Help me to begin to-day."

SERMON VI

MUSIC AND RELIGION [1]

"And I heard as it were the voice of a great multitude, and as the voice of many waters, and as the voice of mighty thunderings, saying, Alleluia! for the Lord God Omnipotent reigneth."—REV. xix. 6.

IF I were asked to give evidence that our Creator has formed us so that it is natural for us to sympathise with one another and easy to work together, I should not appeal to any of those wonders of prehistoric times, such as the pyramids of Egypt, which, no doubt, were raised by the co-operation of a vast number of men; nor should I appeal to the engineering marvels of our own age, its viaducts, its tunnels, its canals. It would seem hardly relevant to cite anything produced by the forced labour of slaves; and even, in other cases, it might be said that men joined to work together rather on account of the great usefulness of the result to be attained than on account of their pleasure in each other's society. I have often thought that the most striking illustration of human sympathy and human co-operation was to be found in a great orchestral chorus. There, perhaps

[1] Preached at the dedication of the cathedral organ of St Mary the Virgin, Southwell, 13th October 1892.

hundreds are united in common work, under no compulsion, but from the pleasure they take in the work itself; no abiding result of the work is to be obtained, all perishes the moment it has been produced, yet in no common work is the discipline so strict. At the appointed instant of time the prescribed sound must be produced by all; its tone is regulated for them: as to its loudness or softness they must obey orders; disobedience in any of these points would spoil the whole effect. If, for example, at a moment when all ought to be silent, a single voice were heard, the offender would incur the indignation not only of the conductor, but of all his companions.

If it be asked what induces so many people to submit to such discipline for the sake of a result so short-lived, the question suggests many reflections. The obvious answer is that it is on account of the pleasure they all feel in the concord of sweet sounds. Yet it must be remarked that the capacity for such pleasure was but of late development in the history of our race, and that it is still very far from being universal—I might almost say from being general.

The element of music that seems to have first developed itself is that of time. A rhythmically recurring beat is a thing which the ear soon learns to catch and be pleased with, and at the present day the uncultured find most pleasure either in dance music in which the beat is strongly marked, or in those parts of music of a different kind at which they find themselves involuntarily beating time. Melody, no doubt, began with the measured repetition of some few very simple phrases; but it could not fail to be observed what intensity was given them when the same strain was sounded by the voices of many. Thus was developed the music of the second Temple, in which the lead of a single voice was followed by a choral response. A notable specimen of such a composition has been preserved for us in Psalm cxxxvi., in which each phrase of the leader of the choir is succeeded by their answer, "For His mercy endureth for ever." And we need not doubt that Purcell, in the anthem we have heard, has rightly interpreted the intention of the close of Psalm cvi., where the exhortation of the leader, "Let all the people say Amen," is obeyed by the pealing Amen of the full chorus. From the Jewish ritual the Amen passed into the Christian, of which it formed one of the most striking parts. What more than one writer has told us of the thunder of the Christian Amen shows that it was not left to be understood or muttered, as so often with us, but was simultaneously pronounced with a loud voice by every member of the congregation.

Both among the Jews and the early Christians the choral singing was altogether unison. It is described in 2 Chron. v. 13, "The trumpeters and singers were as one, to make one sound to be heard in praising and thanking the Lord." The appreciation of harmony came much later, and even still it is far less general than that of melody. And there is nothing which is so changed by culture. The performance of a symphony which is reverenced as a masterpiece by the cultured few, is felt to be a painful weariness by the many.

Now, in tracing this little history of the growth

of musical perception, my object was to bring out this principle, that you must not deny that any faculty is a real part of human nature, either because it is late in its evolution, or because it exhibits itself in some either feebly or almost not at all. He who created the seed foresaw and intended the plant that grows from it, of which He is equally the author, whether he brings it into life full-grown or by slow development. The great progress of physical science has so advanced our knowledge of everything material, that many have come to feel as if nothing except what can be weighed and measured deserved to be accounted real, or were worth our study. In particular, the whole sphere of religion, with its hopes and fears about the Unseen, has been derided as a cloud-born dreamland, and all the affections which faith has called forth have been treated as the mere offspring of superstition. It is, therefore, not amiss to point out how much there is in man that cannot be weighed or measured, and how many faculties of his nature display themselves in the course of his evolution, which the most thorough knowledge of his material structure could not have enabled the most skilful anatomist to predict.

The test of reality is whether our experience corresponds with that of others. The persuasions of a madman may be known to be delusions because his fancies are not shared by those around him. But no one is practically affected by the questions metaphysicians have raised as to how we can have certainty of the existence of the external world around us. "What can we know except our own sensations? How can we tell that there is any

external object corresponding to them? for we seem
to be as certain that there is when we dream as when
we are awake." Yet the common consent of mankind,
in whom similar sensations inspire like convictions,
assures us that to doubt would be insanity. And now
apply this test of reality to the illustration I have
used. Suppose that what we call an ear for music
were as rare as it is now common: suppose that but
one man possessed it, how easily he might have been
made ashamed of his pretensions, and might even
himself doubt whether he were not yielding to a fond
imagination. If he were asked whether he pretended
to have a keener sense of hearing than others, he
might have to own that the case was precisely the
reverse. Again, he might have to own himself quite
ignorant of the philosophy of sound, or of the
structure of the organs of hearing, and might find
that those over whom he claimed superiority could
teach him much that he did not know as to the rate
at which sound travels, and as to the theory of the
vibrations by which it is conveyed. He could hardly
deny that these philosophers had a right to scoff at
his pretensions to find something more than they
knew of in sounds, the whole theory of which they so
thoroughly understood. It requires great strength
of mind to be able to retain one's convictions in the
teeth of nearly universal adverse opinion.

But, on the other hand, how firm our conviction that
our beliefs and our emotions are well-justified when
we find them shared by multitudes. Thus, how idle
were it now to suggest doubts as to the reality of
musical perceptions. The question is practically
settled by the mere fact that it is possible to bring a

number of performers together who feel that they are
well rewarded both for the years of study it has cost
them to acquire their skill, and for the labour of preparation for that particular occasion, by the pleasure
the performance gives them, intensified by their
knowledge of the pleasure felt by their fellow-
workers, whose sympathy assures them that their
consciousness of the capacity for such pleasure is not
a subjective imagination of their own ; but, on the
contrary, that the want of this capacity is a defect
for which a man deserves to be pitied as if he were
born blind.

Now this capacity for musical perception is but
one of several capacities, slow, no doubt, of development, and greatly alterable by culture, but which
prove themselves to have real roots in man's nature
by the facility with which they grow, and the readiness with which they are communicated by one man
to another. There is the awaking of the sense of
natural beauty, whether in scenery, or in form, or in
colour ; there is the power of appreciating the excellence of imitative art in painting or sculpture ; there
is the perception of the harmony of fitly-chosen
spoken words ; there is sensitiveness to the charm
of poetry, and how wide-spread that sensitiveness
is among civilised men, all English-speaking people
have been made to feel this week.[1] Time would fail
me if I attempted to enumerate the capacities
which are the sources of the greatest pleasures of
civilised man, of which his bodily frame gives no
indication.

Man's bodily frame is, indeed, a wonderful piece of

[1] It was the week of Tennyson's death.

mechanism.   Paley and other writers on natural
theology have dwelt on the various contrivances
(for we can use no better word) by which each
part is adapted to the work it has to do.   In this
respect man is an animal like others, for there is no
animal whose bodily structure does not exhibit a like
complexity of arrangements, fitting it for the sphere
it has to occupy.   But there is something that puts a
difference between man and other animals.   We
call it reason, and philosophers thought they had
adequately defined man by describing him as a
rational animal.

Reason is certainly a wonderful faculty.   By it
man has gained dominion over every living thing that
moves upon the earth, and rules over animals immensely superior to himself in strength and swiftness.
By it he rules over the powers of nature, and commands the sea to bear his ships, the sun to paint
his pictures, the lightning to carry his messages.
Nor is reason limited to serving the utilities of man.
It satisfies his thirst for knowledge of the causes of
things, even of those with which we have no practical
concern.   It weighs the sun and the moon, measures
their distances, and searches into the chemical composition of stars.

But this word reason goes a short way in describing the distinguishing faculties of man.   What shall
we say of conscience, the ruler of conduct, which
discriminates right and wrong, which commands, forbids, and, if it is disobeyed, rebukes and punishes ?
If we say that this faculty may fitly be included
under the name of reason, what shall we say of the
feelings generated in one who obeys his conscience,

the indignation against wrong-doing, the loathing of what is mean, or base, or impure? And when I speak of feelings, what a field does that open up! The happiness of man, as we know it, depends on his being capable of affection and love ; it is these that give life all its colour ; without them there could be but one answer to the question, Is life worth living?

And not to make my enumeration too long, I come to speak of faith, the author of all the greatest deeds that have been done in the world ; for it is the strong conviction that faith inspires, a conviction which forcibly communicates itself to others, which has given men courage to attempt tasks apparently beyond their strength, to despise obstacles apparently insurmountable, and which has rewarded their belief by giving them the power it taught them to venture to assume, and by letting them find that in the face of such power, obstacles melt away. And especially we know faith as the evidence of things not seen, which, by revealing a world beyond what sense discloses, opens a new sphere for our feelings and affections. When we come to know of a bene-factor to whom we owe every blessing we have yet received, and on whom our future happiness depends, we feel that our Father which is in Heaven is entitled to a tribute of gratitude and love beyond that which we pay to an earthly father. In this way take their origin all that wide circle of emotions to which we give the name of religion, which have played so leading a part in the history of our race; for what would be a history of mankind if it were silent as to the history of their religions?

I have chosen to speak of our capacity for the religious affections in connection with our sensibility to music, or poetry, or art, because we thus see in a moment the answer to many difficulties and objections. Thus, if it were contended that religion is not natural to man because some savage tribes seem scarcely to know of the existence of a God, or because religion has often been disfigured by debasing superstitions, it might as well be said that our pleasure in music or art was unreal because of the hideous sounds which some savage tribes accept as music, or the tawdry or disgusting disfigurements which they imagine to be ornamental. These rude beginnings bear testimony to tendencies or desires in our constitution which we find our Creator intended should be improved and refined by cultivation and knowledge.

Again, while some have made the foundation of all morality to be our belief that its rules are the commands of a Divine Lawgiver who can enforce these commands by a terrible sanction of future rewards and punishment; others have contended that the conduct of mankind would be little affected if all belief in God, or in a future life, were swept away. To me it seems of small importance how that controversy might be decided. If any one were to say that it is of no consequence whether or not parents were so constituted as to love their children; that reason alone would induce them to take all needful care of them; that in many cases parental love has sadly failed as a stimulus to duty; that children, on the whole, would be as well cared for if the State took charge of them, providing for them education and training, better, in many cases, than that which their parents now give them: however plausible a case might be made out, would you think it worth while to discuss whether it would be advantageous that the family affections should be banished from the world? In like manner, it would be idle to discuss whether or not the religious affections can be defended on the ground of their utility, because, for instance, they serve as a sanction to morality, or because they are good for anything else. These affections in themselves constitute the happiness of multitudes of our fellow-creatures. To many they furnish the whole poetry of life, the one thing that lifts their thoughts above the drudging toil necessary to gain their daily bread.

No doubt, men who enjoy great material prosperity find it easy to forget God, for the time feeling little need of the consolations of religion. So in like manner we may know of men so absorbed in money getting, which seems to them the one important thing, that they despise such frivolities as literature and art. But can you think that such men choose the better part?

But let sorrow come, as it must to everybody, sickness, danger, bereavement, then it is known what hope and strength religion can supply. I am old enough to remember the discussions about slavery in America before the great Civil War put an end to it; and I believe we ought not to leave out of the account that, for the sufferings that some of them had to endure, the Negro race had received two compensations in having been educated in music and in Christianity. With their hymns, and with the hopes that these hymns expressed, with all their enforced toil, they were, on the whole, not an unhappy race.

But, thank Heaven, there are millions who do not wait until earthly happiness fails before learning to know the happiness of communion with a Father who loves them, a Saviour who died for them. Such communion gives all the brightness to their lives. You might say that it would be a colourless world if it were a world without music, a world without art, a world without poetry; but there could be no such dismal world as a world without God.

And yet, as I said before, our nature is such that it is almost impossible to maintain a solitary conviction in the teeth of surrounding disbelief. So God has provided that our faith in Him should not be solitary; and Christ, by the institution of His Church, has ordained that our faith should be invigorated, cheered, justified by the sympathy of fellow partakers in the same exceeding great and precious promises, who, living the same life of faith, can testify to us that their experience of its fruits is the same as ours. The New Testament does not regard any Christian as isolated from the rest; each is but a living stone intended to form part of a holy temple in the Lord, built on the foundation of the apostles and prophets, Jesus Christ Himself being the chief Corner Stone, the whole fabric to constitute a habitation of God through the Spirit. Elsewhere another comparison is used, and the Church is described as a living organism; a body of which Christ is the Head; each individual Christian a member; the members having, according to their station, their independent functions, but all so bound in sympathy to each other that if one member suffer all the members suffer with it ; if one member be honoured all the members rejoice with it.

Thus Christ has ordained that His people should lead no isolated lives. St Paul speaks of each making melody in his heart to the Lord. But Christ has further provided that the melody should become a harmony—not the feeble utterance of a single voice, but swelled by the concert of multitudes to become, as it is described in the text, as the voice of many waters, as the voice of mighty thunderings. Perhaps then, it is not fanciful, as it is certainly appropriate to the day, to see a type of the Church in the great organ which is especially the instrument of harmony.

Wind instruments had been long in use, and it was an obvious invention to have the wind produced by mechanical means instead of by the human breath ; but as long as only melody was cared for, this could be satisfied with something of the nature of the bagpipes. It was not until the sense of harmony fully awoke that it was sought to combine many instruments into one, so as to enable a full harmony to be produced by a single player.

It is remarkable how the organ, which was entirely secular in its origin, has been almost completely won over to sacred uses. It must be owned that in the early ages of the Christian Church instrumental music was not used in the worship of God, as it still is not in the East. It was entirely for secular purposes the organ was invented. Of this we have a curious illustration in the legend of St Caecilia. Her story tells that, though she had dedicated herself to a life of virginity, she was compelled to go through the

ceremony of marriage with a noble young Roman,
whom, however, she prevailed on to respect her vows,
whereupon he was privileged to see the angel who
guarded her. Her legend, in its original form, describes the allurements to worldly pleasure which she
had to resist, dwelling, in particular, on the music of
the nuptial feast, and specially of the organ, to which
she resolutely shut her ears. Now the necessities of
the pictorial art demanded that in order that it should
be known what particular saint was intended, the
representation of each should be accompanied with
its appropriate sign, which, in the case of a martyr,
was usually the instrument of torture by which he
suffered. So St Paul was represented with his sword,
St Laurence with his gridiron, St Catherine with her
wheel. Thus, St Caecilia was represented with the
organ and the angel which so prominently figured in
her story. Afterwards, when the organ had been
quite gained over from secular to ecclesiastical uses,
the picture suggested the idea that Caecilia's skill in
sounding the praises of God upon the organ had
drawn down an angel to listen to her music. If in
this instance a mistake was made, it was one which
sprang out of an idea for which higher authority can
be pleaded, the idea that angels are not indifferent to
men's worship of Him who is God over men and
angels, the idea that there may be sympathy between
the praises of men on earth and those of the heavenly
host. I will not cite two or three passages of Scripture which will rise to your recollection, but you know
how early the Church adopted into her service the
" Holy, Holy, Holy " which the prophet described as
the cry of the Heavenly Host, and delighted to think

that her children were uniting their earthly hallelujahs to those of angels and archangels, and all the company of Heaven.

There is great moral significance in the fact that while Scripture gives no answer to many curious questions we might ask as to the occupation of the Blessed hereafter, it at least represents them as joining in singing the praises of God and of the Lamb ; their habitual frame as one of loving worship of Him by whom they were redeemed, and of perfect harmony with each other. And I believe that the reason why the pleasures of music may be fitly associated in our minds with the joys of Heaven is because, as I said at the beginning, nowhere else do we find so striking an illustration of the power of a multitude of human wills united in one harmonious whole. God has so constituted us that man does not attain the highest state of which he is capable until each has learned to subordinate his own will to the wills of others, such a union of wills being not only the necessary means of our protection from danger, but the source of our purest pleasure. And when the object of this union of human wills is the sounding forth the glory of God, earth can afford no symbol which more fully expresses the enjoyment of Heaven.

The illustration of an orchestral chorus exhibits what diversity there may be in the instruments which united make harmony. In the Church the instruments that make up the harmony are not only diverse, but sometimes discordant. But the organ shows that discords may contribute to harmony. For when each note is sounded with the harmonics that accompany it, a theorist might pronounce that a chord could not be sounded without inevitable discord. Yet it is found that these small discords overpowered do but add to the fulness and richness of the harmony. Sometimes we who stand too near have ears only for the discords, and cannot appreciate the general effect. When men differ with us, it may be on points by no means essential, we find it hard to give them credit for sincere love to Christ, and when they are in nominal union with ourselves would, perhaps, be little grieved if they were to part from us altogether. But the more we strive that our love to Christ shall be genuine, and not merely disguised love for our own way, the more quick shall we be to recognise the same love in others.

And O brethren, would it not be a heaven upon earth if we were all animated with one will, and that will God's will ! You may make your whole earthly life an anthem to the praise of God if each of you, setting before you the glory of God as your principle of conduct, strive to promote that glory by harmonious action with each other, following after the things which make for peace, praying for the peace of our Jerusalem, striving by your lives to earn the glorious title which our Lord has given to the peacemakers—the Children of God.

SERMON VII

COLOUR-BLINDNESS

"Having eyes see ye not? and having ears hear ye not? and do ye not remember?"—MARK viii. 18.

IT is strange how easy it is to fail to see things that are right before one's eyes. Taking these words in the most literal sense, it is common enough to find men, either from want of keenness of vision, or more frequently from want of trained powers of observation, failing to notice things quite obvious, and which, when once their attention has been called to them, they themselves can hardly understand how they could ever have overlooked. And this is still more true when we use the word "seeing" to denote mental perception. Hardly ever has a great discovery been made but it is remarked how near to it several predecessors of the real discoverer had been. They had gone so near it that it seems almost incredible that they should not have gone the little further way that made all the difference between failure and success.

The fact is, that we are constantly forced to recognise the limitations of human faculties. I do not so much mean when the faculties of man are compared with those of other animals; but I want to speak to you to-day of gifts that the experience of others shows that man might possess, and that are lost for want of attention and cultivation. There are diversities of power between one man and another depending on natural gifts, which sometimes puzzle us as to whether we ought to regard one man as exceptionally gifted or to pronounce others to be abnormally defective. I remember that a friend of mine, himself a good arithmetician, met in the west of England an elderly man who in his youth had exhibited as a calculating boy, being able to give instantaneous answers to complicated arithmetical problems which would take an ordinary calculator perhaps half-an-hour to work out on paper. My friend asked him to explain how he was able to do it. He said: "I cannot explain; the only thing I cannot understand is how it is that you are not able to do it." Something of the same kind may be said of those powers of instantaneous combination which were possessed by the first Napoleon, which not only no general of his day, but perhaps not two or three in the history of the world, were able to reach. Yet there seems no reason why those gifts which are now exceptional might not have been more widely distributed—nay, so widely that to be without them might seem to come as short of the ordinary heritage of humanity as to be born deaf or dumb. Every one of those endowments which exceptional men enjoy is a revelation to us of the possibilities of things, and shows us what God might have given to all as He has given to some; nay, possibly what He intends that all should grow unto, and designs to make the general possession of the race.

Now, in real truth, we find there are gifts well within man's power to obtain that many are without only because they have not cared to cultivate them. Take, for example, the sense of beauty, and see how it has been developed by culture. Many animals surpass us in keenness of vision. I don't know whether any man can compare in that respect with a greyhound or a hawk. No doubt a horse or a cow can see everything in a landscape that we can see, and if the animal discerns grass or anything else of practical utility to him, no doubt the sight gives him pleasure. But the power of feeling delight in the beauty of a landscape for its own sake we may regard as a specially human endowment, if, indeed, we can give that name to what all men do not possess. Indeed, I doubt if children, as a general rule, show signs of it. In fact, during the century now coming to a close, the feeling of delight in the contemplation of Nature has received so much development that mankind may be almost said to have developed a new faculty. Men whose faculties are entirely engrossed with providing sustenance for themselves and their families, or with guarding against impending dangers, have no leisure for admiration of scenery. Times were when districts, whose loveliness or whose grandeur now annually brings to innkeepers a golden harvest of tourists, were hastily passed through by anxious travellers with no eye for tree or rock save to ascertain that it did not furnish a shelter for some plunderer. Times were when the Alps, now the playground of Europe, were regarded as a hideous excrescence on the face of Nature, wastefully occupying space which a more kindly Providence would have reserved for verdant pastures or waving corn.

Even though many men, whose æsthetic suscepti-bilities are but small, would hesitate to acknowledge that they have no enjoyment of scenery—at least there are many who would frankly own that they have no ear for music, which one of them has ventured to call the least disagreeable of noises. That is a gift which if our Creator had left us without, nobody would have missed, or even dreamed that he wanted anything necessary to life or happiness. Yet those who possess it recognise it as a new faculty, opening to us through the gratuitous bounty of our Maker a new source of rational enjoyment. It is a faculty which very few are absolutely without, if they care to cultivate it, but there is no faculty which is more developed by cultivation, so that one learns to perceive beauty, and find a source of pleasure, in what would once have been a wearisome infliction. Even in our own century taste has greatly changed, and it is, not only in poetry but in music, that compositions which are now most admired, received, at the beginning of the century, from the critics then in the highest esteem, the verdict—This will never do.

Any one who thought that he knew all that was in man would be surprised at discovering the suc-cessive evolution of new faculties—we might almost say new senses. Many illustrations might be given; but as I have spoken as to the difference of percep-tion of musical sounds between men all equally gifted with the sense of hearing, so it is natural to say something of the corresponding difference between men equally gifted with the sense of sight. The

F

possibility of colour-blindness is really a discovery of our own century. It was then found out that some men, by no means inferior to their fellows in keenness of sight, failed to perceive differences of colour. In truth, the case completely corresponds to the absence of an ear for music—the one defect arising from incapacity of being affected by differences in the velocity of waves of light, the other in that of the waves of sound. It is so natural to us to imagine (though the thing is incapable of absolute proof) that our fellow-men experience from the same sources exactly the same sensations as ourselves, that it easily long escaped notice, that this is by no means universally the case, as far as the perception of colour is concerned. And the discovery was little attended to as long as it was thought that the defect merely imposed the loss of a pleasure, and until it was found that there were certain useful services which the defect renders a man unable to render, so that modern care finds it necessary to guard against incompetence by test examinations. But considered merely as a source of pleasure, how much is lost by one who is without this sense? How much are we indebted to the bounty of our Creator, who has clothed Nature with its attire of many-changing hues, and has given us the faculty of discerning them? How dull would the face of Nature be if she wore always one sombre uniform dress! If we knew nothing of the gay brilliancy of flowers, of the varied tints of autumn foliage, of the gorgeous colouring of a summer sunset! If the painter's art could express no more to us than that of the sculptor! If we knew no more of the features of those we love than can be made known to us by an uncoloured photograph!

The fact is, that the more we study man the more we find what a very complex being he is. New faculties are constantly starting to light, and old ones receive such new developments by cultivation that we can hardly set limits to the possible future endowments of the race.

Let me, for example, remind you that there is such a thing as a moral sense—that is to say, a faculty of perceiving moral relations. There is scarcely any one absolutely without it. Yet there are many who seem to be so, in the eyes of those who have cultivated the faculty more assiduously than they. There is scarcely any of us, however well he may be trying to do his duty according to his lights, who might not be addressed with "having eyes see ye not?" by those who have attained a higher moral standard, and see us neglecting duties, which, according to their view, are plain before our eyes. We may believe this to be true of ourselves because we are often tempted to say it of our ancestors, among whom were many as resolved as we can be to obey the dictates of their conscience, and yet whose consciences never told them of things that are plain to ours. I suppose that in the earlier stages of civilisation men were thought sufficiently virtuous if they abstained from those gross violations of the rights of others which are forbidden in the sixth, seventh, and eighth commandments. But as time went on, Christians became more and more alive to all that was included in their Master's precepts ; "Thou shalt love the Lord thy God with all thy heart, and all thy soul, and all thy strength, and thy neighbour as thyself," "Do unto all men as ye would they should do unto you;" and who shall say that we have yet exhausted all that is meant by these commands? The most important of them have been embodied in human laws, and are enforced by public opinion. Yet they are often transgressed by men who would be sorry not to be thought virtuous and honest. Sometimes, in their attempts to advance their own interests, they commit actions which when reviewed by a court of equity are condemned as illegal. If they escape that condemnation, they get a reputation for sharp practice, the cleverness of which, in this country at least, is not thought sufficient justification. There are those who in their intercourse with others try to exalt their own reputation by extravagant self-laudation, or by depreciation of possible rivals, and are so dense as not to perceive that their exertions to make themselves stand higher in the esteem of others, have really the effect of lessening the respect with which they are regarded ; for it is strange how grudgingly praise that we would freely have bestowed spontaneously, is given when it seems to be extorted from us by one who cares for it. Only in one point do I perceive that practical morality is declining at the present day. There are those who are colour blind with respect to moral beauty. All other kinds of beauty they can appreciate, but morality has no place in their science of æsthetics, and they can give their praise to works of art without being in the least repelled by their moral hideousness.

But there is one more part of our complex nature of which it was my principal object to speak to-day, and, as far as our happiness is concerned, it is one of the most important—I mean the emotional part. Could we own a being as a man, who had no capacity for hope and fear, pity, admiration, reverence, love? It is these emotions which give life its colour and stimulate most of its actions. But there is none of them which has so moved the simultaneous actions of large bodies of men as those whose object is the common Father of all—He who is most worthy of reverence, whose power inspires the greatest awe, who can hold out the most alluring hopes or the most terrible fears, whose bounty draws forth the strongest love. To gain the favour of such a Being must naturally be the highest aim of humanity, to know that one enjoys it, the greatest earthly happiness. This knowledge has been to millions a fountain of abiding peace not to be disturbed by any of the vicissitudes of life; in times of prosperity heightening the enjoyment with the thought that it is a Father's gift, and in times of adversity also bringing consolation with the same thought, that this, too, comes from a Father who loves us, and is wiser than we to discern what is really good for us. Thus it is that the tyranny of men cannot frighten one who knows that there is with him One stronger than any that can be against him. Thus it is that privation and painful sickness can be borne cheerfully as sent by One who loves us and does not afflict willingly; that the sorrow of bereavement loses its bitterness when it is known that He who takes away is the same as He who has given, and can also reunite. Heaviness may endure for a night, but joy cometh in the morning. What shall we say of those who are without the capacity for entertaining these feelings? for it is the unhappy lot of some.

The ideas which I have been dwelling on to-day were suggested to me by a story told me by my late friend, Professor Haughton, not long before he died. He had had with Professor Huxley a friendship the warmth of which was not affected by their wide differences in religious opinion. Huxley one day said to him: "There are those who profess to believe what I consider to be false; but I do not regard their opinions, because I doubt the sincerity of some and the intellectual capacity of others; but I respect you, and I know how sincerely you believe what you hold so strongly, and should like very much to know how it is that you believe what I can't believe." "May I speak frankly?" said Haughton. "Certainly," said he. "Then," he said, "I don't know how it is, except that you are colour-blind." Huxley was much struck. He said, "Well, it may be so. Of course, if I were colour-blind, I should not know it myself."

And surely it were a great misfortune to be born without a faculty from which others derive their highest pleasures. Yet that is a calamity which need bring no self-reproach. But what if the same talent had been committed to us as to the rest, and that it was only through our own remissness that it had disappeared? For every one of the faculties of which I have been speaking, obeys the general law that it can be strengthened and improved by use, but becomes atrophied by neglect. As a general rule, those who are most deficient in these faculties were not born without them; the most backward had them, at least, in a rudimentary state, and if they had not been inattentive to their perceptions, might have developed them by cultivation. More especially is this the case with those who are so absorbed in objects of sense as to have no care for anything which the bodily eye cannot see nor bodily organs handle. Then the perceptions which they neglect become fainter as not attended to, until at length they fancy there is nothing real in anything that the eye of faith reveals. But what is the test of reality? It is that other people can share our experience. We reject the imaginations of a dream as unreal, because no one but ourselves has perception of them; but are those things unreal which constitute the happiness of the lives of thousands?

We can conceive it as a singular privilege to be granted an eagle eye to take knowledge of things which the dim-seeing multitude are insensible of. But what a gift is that on which some pride themselves—to be able NOT to see what is quite clear to their fellows. Are there any of you who covet that melancholy privilege: having eyes to see not; having ears not to understand; who think themselves superior to their fellows because of being able not to see what is quite clear to them?

SERMON VIII

THE COLOUR-BLINDNESS OF JUDAS

"Yea, mine own familiar friend in whom I trusted, which did eat of my bread, hath lifted up his heel against me."—PSALM xli. 9.

WE recognise in these words of the Psalmist a prophecy of Judas Iscariot; and we have our Lord's own authority for doing so; for St John (xiii. 18) tells us how our Lord at His last supper so applied this utterance of the Psalmist. It is of that traitor apostle that I am about to speak to you to-day. You may wonder at my thinking to find in his history subject for profitable meditation. It is true that in our struggles with temptation there is no more edifying study than that of the lives of other men, in order that we may profit by the example of those who have triumphed over the temptations that assail ourselves, or be warned by the fate of those who have yielded to them. But in order to gain this edification, the lives that we study must be those of men, not of angels or demons; neither of beings who are without those tendencies to evil of which we are ourselves conscious, nor of those whose moral state is so low as to inspire only horror and repulsion.

Our natural feeling would be to refer Judas to the latter class; but there are two kinds of spirit in which the history of a bad man may be studied. One is that of the prayer of the Pharisee in the parable: "God, I thank Thee that I am not as other men," for it is very common to judge oneself, not by comparison with God's law, but with the average conduct of our neighbours, a method by which it is much easier to obtain a favourable verdict.

The other spirit in which the history of a bad man may be studied is that of Richard Baxter, according to the story which represents him as saying when he saw a criminal led to execution: "There goes Richard Baxter if it had not been for the grace of God." In other words, he was conscious of tendencies in himself which, if God had not given him grace to check and overcome them, would have led him even into crimes which human laws cannot leave unpunished.

There is no moral gain from taking pride in reflecting how much better we are than some who have incurred deserved disgrace; but there may be much from observing his points of likeness with ourselves, so that we may take warning if we beguile our own consciences with the same devices which were successful in silencing his.

But it will probably be thought an extreme case if I attempt to draw such a lesson from the perpetrator of the greatest crime in human history; whose name is the most opprobrious that any could fasten on the greatest reprobate. No one would pride himself in being a better man than Judas, though he might be shocked at being told that he was not so much better as he thought himself. It is because I am persuaded that if Judas tried himself by his own standards he would not have thought himself a bad man, that I think it profitable to enquire why we hate his name, and to examine into the pleas by which he might have excused his conduct to himself, the result being that when we have disposed of all his imagined justifications, we find remaining as the source of all his wickedness, only an evil in a magnified form which lurks in all our hearts.

Now, I am not going to follow the example of some ingenious men who delight in reversing popular judgments : in picking holes in the characters of men whose lives have been the subject of popular admiration ; and in showing that others who have been branded as villains have been unjustly condemned, and that even if they had actually committed the deeds laid to their charge, they had some virtuous or honourable motive.

A good many years ago an attempt was made to clear Judas from the imputation of treachery prompted by sordid avarice. The idea of the speculation was that Judas had been greatly impressed by the miracles of his Master, and was fully persuaded of His divine power—that he imagined that if our Lord would only use the power He possessed, He could overthrow the Roman dominion, and make Israel the chief of nations—that having joined Jesus in the hope of sharing in the prizes of His success, and being disappointed and disgusted at the delay of the fulfilment of his expectations, he tried to bring matters to a crisis, persuaded that if his Master were reduced to choose between putting forth His supernatural power or allowing His life to be sacrificed, He would no longer hesitate, and His triumph would be assured. And then the speculation goes on to explain the result, how Judas, horror-struck at the event of his project, which, instead of gaining victory for his cause, disclosed him to himself as one who for money had betrayed innocent blood, could not bear the thought, and went and hanged himself. In other words, according to this theory, we are to think of Judas, not so much as of one who committed a crime, as of one who, unfortunately, made a miscalculation.

It is a fatal flaw in this beautiful theory that it is so modern. The survivors of his fellow disciples show no gratitude for his mistaken zeal; and in the few and restrained words in which the Evangelists tell his story, they exhibit only a natural loathing for the baseness of his treachery. And if I could adopt the modern view, I should not regard the story as a subject for profitable meditation. For what lesson can we well draw from the conduct of a man in difficult circumstances such as we are never likely to be placed in? The only lesson that I see to draw from it is, "Thou shalt not do evil that good may come."

If I speak of Judas as not so much worse than ordinary men as you might have supposed, it is not with the wish to make you think better of him, but to make you think less confidently of yourselves. For there is a lesson that we may found on the text: "Let him that thinketh he standeth take heed lest he fall," if we consider what Judas was before his great sin, when, no doubt, he would have been thought as little likely to be a great criminal as any ordinary member of a respectable church congregation. He could not have been an irreligious man, or he would never have been admitted into the society of the

Twelve; and it is clear that the other apostles had full confidence in him. He was, in fact, made the treasurer of their little community, having (no doubt deservedly) the reputation of an able and clear-headed as well as of a good man. It speaks well for him that he was attracted by our Lord, and sought admission into His company. And if it be the case that he was misled by the expectation of finding in his Master one who would soon be the dispenser of temporal wealth and power, the expectation was common to him with the other disciples. To the last they went on speculating and disputing with each other the distribution of high places in the coming kingdom; and even after the Resurrection we learn from St Luke that the apostles were eager to know *when* it was that Jesus would restore the kingdom to Israel. There is no doubt that in the last journey to Jerusalem, St Peter and some other of the apostles were persuaded that the Kingdom of God, in the sense in which they looked for it, would immediately appear. The triumphal entry into Jerusalem, and the proclamation of their Leader as the Son of David, must have been felt on both sides as a challenge to the then ruling powers; and those who so often had witnessed the supernatural power of Jesus, could feel no doubt as to the result of any conflict their challenge might provoke. It was in vain that their Master told them that their enterprise would but end in an ignominious death for Himself. This was to His eager disciples simply incredible; they thought that He must be using words in some mysterious sense.

And if there was one man of their body with too

of Jesus, had seen His mighty acts, had heard His gracious words; yet all His wisdom, all His goodness, had met no appreciation. Judas, no doubt, could boast of being a clear-sighted man, who saw things as they really were, and was not misled by the illusive dreams of which the heads of his brethren were full. How was it that they could see what he could not see, and had faculties capable of recognising the greatness of a Master whom he only despised as a mistaken enthusiast? It is this absolute deadness of spiritual perception which I count to be the radical flaw in the character of Judas; and to be that which makes the study of his history really profitable for our example and warning. It is a very exceptional thing that one of us should be under a temptation to anything that may be called treachery; but we may all do well to bear in mind that what made the fall of Judas possible was that he was clear-sighted with respect to material objects, and to all the things of this life, but that the spiritual world was quite invisible to him.

In comparison with this, I have not thought it worth while to dwell on what, to our modern feelings, is most shocking in Judas's desertion of his Master— namely, that he took money for doing it. I call it a modern feeling, because, undoubtedly, there is now a delicacy of feeling as to the circumstances under which it is right to accept money which did not exist in earlier times. I suppose there never could have been a time, since moral judgments were made at all, when it could have been thought right to take money for doing a wrong thing which was also injurious to another person. But suppose the thing done was

G

innocent and right, it was easy to think that there was nothing wrong in receiving a pecuniary acknowledgment from one who had benefited by it. It is not so long since a judge, who had decided in favour of the side on which he believed the merits to lie, did not scruple to receive the deserved tribute by which the grateful suitor acknowledged his sagacity; not so long since a statesman who had given a public contract to one well qualified to carry it out, thought it quite fair that he should share the profits which his wise choice had enabled his *protégé* to make; not so long since British statesmen were pensioners of the French king, and an apologetic historian tells us that they certainly would not have taken money to injure their country, though it was, no doubt, a little indelicate that they should allow a foreigner to pay them for serving her.

We could hardly expect a poor Jew, at the beginning of our era, to have discovered that the reasons which were enough to justify his action would not also justify his taking money for doing it. If he had convinced himself that, in the interests of law and order, and in order to save the lives of his companions, it was right that he should give his help in privately capturing the claimant to the Throne of David, he could hardly be expected to refuse the reward for his services which the Government was willing to give. We have not the means of calculating the value of that reward in the money of our day, but it must have been considerable, for the sum was too large to be spent; it had to be invested, and was enough to make Judas a landed proprietor (*see* Acts i. 18). The earliest uncanonical tradition about Judas would make us think of the interval before his death as not a very short one. It would be a mistake to ascribe much authority to such traditions; but possibly we may also be mistaken in inferring from the story, as told by St Matthew, that the repentance of Judas followed immediately on his crime. If David could not help murmuring when he saw the wicked in prosperity, what must the apostles have felt if they saw the traitor a rich and prosperous citizen?

You would greatly misunderstand me if you thought that the object of this discourse was to make apologies for Judas. If I try to show that he was not so much worse than one of yourselves as you might have imagined, it is not with the intention of making you think better of him, but worse of yourselves. When all that can be said for Judas has been said, the fact remains that he had been for months in close companionship with One than whom none who ever trod this earth was more worthy of love and reverence, and yet he neither loved Him nor appreciated Him. For all the things of this life he was clear-sighted. He could measure, as his companions could not, the strength of the existing Government, and could see the hopelessness of an attempt to overthrow it. He could approve the wisdom of the Jewish rulers in discouraging any movement that might bring them into collision with the Roman Government. He could well estimate the blood that would be vainly shed in the event of such a collision, and could willingly adopt the high priest's calculation that it was expedient that one man should die that the whole nation perish not. But what his arithmetic could not measure was the value of that single life which he thought little of sacrificing. We cannot but marvel at the blindness of this clear-sighted man. Think what value we should set on the privilege—the worth of which he lightly esteemed—the privilege of being admitted to the intimate companionship of his Master, of being constantly with Jesus as He went about doing good, of hearing all the gracious words that proceeded from His mouth, of being taught by Him how to profit by the traditional teaching of the Scribes, discriminating what in it was true and important from what was arbitrary and worthless, of being enabled to see through the vain shows of earth and discern the realities of the Eternal Kingdom ; and yet, strange to say, the disciple only felt contempt for his Teacher as an unpractical dreamer, deluded by His own visions, and unable to see things as they really were.

The practical question for us now is : Are we to regard the spiritual blindness of Judas as a strange and exceptional defect ; or, is it not rather that the power of spiritual discernment is a faculty of which God has made us capable, but which, with many, remains altogether unawakened ; with others is neglected, stifled, and ultimately lost? Are we not like the Jews of our Lord's time, who were ready to do honour to the memory of the men of former days that had left a high reputation, who were willing to build the sepulchres of the prophets, and could honestly flatter themselves with the boast, " If we had been in the days of our fathers we should not have been partakers with them in the blood of the prophets ;" and yet it was but want of the power of historical imagination that concealed from them the fact that, if they had been in the days of their fathers, they would be likely to have shared in the popular sentiment, and swelled the crowd of the prophets' persecutors? Does it seem to you a monstrous question if I were to ask you : Are you sure that, if you had been in the days of the apostles, you might not have had more admiration for the clear common-sense of Judas than for the moral greatness of Him to whose death he was a party? For, after all, is the faculty of perception of moral greatness so very common ? Go to the busy market-place, and see among the crowd of buyers and sellers how many you would find who would be willing to turn aside from their merchandise to listen to talk which they would deem unprofitable chatter. Would you have more success in private with the sagacious mercantile man, with the successful advocate, with the busy politician? Should you not expect to find all taking their main interest in the things by which this world's wealth or honours could be gained, and counting time to be wasted in speculations which brought no profit ? The majority of mankind trouble themselves little more than the beasts of the field about anything beyond what is necessary for the satisfying of their animal wants. Yet there is latent in all, feeble though it may be in some, the faculty of recognising moral greatness ; and it is strange in what rude breasts the utterance of a noble sentiment, or the recital of a deed of generous self-sacrifice, will stir a sympathetic thrill.

Brethren, see that the light which is in you be not darkness ; for nothing is easier than to quench the struggling glimmer of the heavenly light, which is meant to show you the worlds above. A cynical speech, a scoffing laugh, may shut out your escape from the materialising influences of your common life, just as in the garish light of day you are incapable of discerning the wonders of the starry firmament. We cannot call the cattle miserable because they have no higher conception of happiness than abundant gratification of their animal cravings, for this is all that God has made them capable of; but you, whom God has gifted with a capacity for something higher—namely, with the power in some degree to know Himself, take warning by the example of him who, in his stupid misappreciation of the value of things material and things spiritual, made a mistake so dire that it could be said of him : "Good were it for that man if he had not been born."

SERMON IX

SUPERSTITION

"Then Paul stood in the midst of Mars' hill, and said, Ye men of Athens, I perceive that ye are in all things too superstitious."—ACTS xvii. 22.

IN the Revised Version of the New Testament, the language of the text is somewhat softened. There it runs, "In all things I perceive that ye are somewhat superstitious." But the revisers in their margin suggest a greater change, viz., instead of "superstitious," to read "religious." They had not boldness to introduce the change into their text, and, indeed, it would have been a little awkward if they had either made Paul blame the Athenians for being "too religious," or compliment them for being "somewhat religious." The case is one which always presents a difficulty to translators when they have to deal with a word in one language which has not the same limits of meaning as those of the corresponding word in another. In our language the word superstitious is always used in a bad sense; to us a superstitious man means one possessed with a belief which is certainly false and foolish, and possibly even mischievous; the word "religious," on the other hand, is always used in a good sense; and we mean a compliment if we say of any one that he is a religious man: for the only religion we recognise is the worship of a God who hates all iniquity, and will show favour to none who cherish evil in their hearts; so that one who can truly be described as religious—that is to say, as making it the habitual aim of his life to try to please this God of Purity, must be one also deserving the love and confidence of men. But the corresponding Greek word which occurs in this text has neither the flavour of commendation which attaches to the word religious, nor does it convey the note of censure which the word superstitious involves. It means little more than one addicted to the reverence of unseen beings.

But what would be the moral value of such reverence among a people who worshipped gods many and lords many; and these, gods who could not be conceived of as lovers of purity and holiness; for concerning themselves stories were told which, though disbelieved and scoffed at by the educated few, were deep-rooted in popular belief, which represented these divinities as guilty of acts of which any decently conducted man would be ashamed — as being so bad that the early Christians were not far wrong in looking on the heathen as worshippers of devils. What would be our own moral condition if we believed that supreme power was possessed by a being thoroughly selfish and capricious if not malignant, and if what we called religion was only a series of contrivances for making this being propitious or, at least, keeping him from doing us overmuch injury? Would it be strange if, where such a belief prevailed, religion and superstition, in the judgment of thoughtful men, should come to mean the same thing? And so in fact it proved. We can read with much sympathy the sublime poem in which an ancient unbeliever professed it to be his aim to remove from off the minds of men the crushing burden under which "religion" was pressing them down, because we see that what he calls religion we should call superstition. When, for example, he recalls a then familiar story, how, when an expedition was detained by long-continued contrary winds, the king, in order to obtain a favourable change, offered his own daughter in sacrifice, we can sympathise with the poet's indignation when he exclaims : " Such are the evils for the suggestion of which religion is responsible ! " because what we honour with the name of religion disclaims all partnership with such guilt.

Now, then, that we understand the ambiguity of the word, the question remains for us, What meaning did Paul wish to convey when he described the Athenians as superstitious ? I think we can safely say that Paul was not at all likely in addressing a strange audience, and *that* one not disposed to be friendly, to begin with a censure or a scoff at their superstition in the sense that we use the word. His method always was not to put his points of difference with his hearers in the front of his discourse, but rather to win their assent by building the fabric of his argument on what he and they held in common. Thus when he wished to gain over his Pharisaic auditors at the Jewish Council, he prepared them to accept his announcement of the resurrection of Jesus by reminding them that on the question whether a resurrection from the dead were possible, the Pharisees and the Christians were united in opposition to the Sadducees. In addressing a Roman governor, he reasoned about righteousness, temperance, and judgment to come: for on these topics he could appeal to what was already written on the conscience of his hearer. But when he was to address a king, well read in the Jewish Scriptures, he uses higher ground which he has in common with him, and cries: "King Agrippa, believest thou the prophets? I know that thou believest." And here, too, he catches at something which his hearers were bound to concede. He says in substance: "I have been accused of being a setter forth of strange Gods. Well, you have been prepared to hear of such. I could not walk round your city without observing a multitude of tokens how addicted to worship you are. Among the objects of your veneration I noted an altar dedicated to the Unknown God. You own, then, that there is a God whom you do not yet know. It is such a One that I have to set forth to you—even the God that made the world and all things therein: the Lord of Heaven and earth." Thus you see that St Paul in his dealings with the Athenians did not proceed by any different method from that which he followed with others whom he desired to convert to Christianity—namely, to take the truths which they already held, and build on them, rather than begin with a direct attack on their errors. It may seem strange to us that after Paul had resided a couple of years at least in Ephesus, the town clerk was able to still the fury of a heated mob against Paul and his party, by reminding them that these men had not been guilty either of sacrilege against their temple, or even of blasphemy against their goddess.

But you will easily understand that I did not choose my text to-day with the intention of discussing the history of the apostle Paul, but rather because its language gives me occasion to speak on a subject I believe to be useful, the necessity of being cautious, lest in the blows we strike against superstition we should wound religion. There are many who would think it a sufficient rule for guiding us into right ideas about religion, to say : "Beware of superstition." Yet we have just seen that when in the New Testament certain people are described as superstitious, commentators are not agreed whether this is meant as a compliment or a censure. I spoke already of the heathen poet in whose language the two words meant the same, who found no way of shaking off the yoke of a religion which inculcated human sacrifices except by teaching that the gods, if gods there were, lived in the enjoyment of their own happiness, and took neither trouble nor interest in human affairs. But, happily, we are not reduced to the necessity of casting away true and false beliefs together indiscriminately, since we find it possible to cast away the false and retain the true.

The question used to be discussed by philosophers which were best, Atheism or Superstition ; and Plutarch declared his decision in favour of Atheism, "For," said he, "I had much rather it was believed that there never had been such a man as Plutarch, than that it were believed that indeed there was such a man, but that he was one who ate his children, who debauched wives and virgins, and did the other abominable things which the popular belief at that time attributed to some of the divinities they worshipped." Truly, if we were reduced to so miserable a choice, we might own it to be better to believe in no god than in a bad god, in a god such as some whose worshippers believed that it was by impurity and bloodshed their divinity could be best propitiated. Surely, if in our battle against falsehood, impurity, and injustice, we found the most powerful being in the universe ranged on the wrong side, we should be delighted to hear that he had taken himself off to epicurean enjoyments of his own, and left the contest to be fairly fought out on even terms. But we are thankful to know that the Most High does rule over the kingdom of men, and that He is on our side, or rather that we are privileged to be on His. This is a truth so precious, that even a large admixture of human errors does not deprive it of its value, and we should pay too high a price for getting rid of these errors if we had to part with the truth as well. Lord Bacon, whom I have quoted already, gives his own verdict on the question between Atheism and Superstition : " I had rather believe all the fables in the 'Legend,' and the 'Talmud' and the 'Alcoran' than that this universal frame is without a mind."

He says, further, that there is a superstition in avoiding superstition, when men think that they do best when they go furthest from the superstition formerly received. And surely nothing can be more natural than that men who have groaned under a tyranny should exceed the bounds of moderation in shaking it off. It was not wonderful that the gross-ness of the heathen fables should produce a reaction in the direction of Atheism, and that thoughtful men, taking note of the evils which false beliefs had wrought, should imagine that the one thing necessary for human happiness was to clear the intellect from error, and reduce belief to things which the senses bear witness to. For it is too much to expect that when men discover that the popular creed is grossly tainted with falsehood they will be so patient as, instead of then rejecting it altogether, to stay to examine carefully what portions of truth it may contain, and then make a discriminating choice, retaining what is good, and casting away the false. What actually is wont to happen is that they begin by casting away the entire, and only find out by trial that they have made a mistake in parting with something that it would be a calamity to lose. Our own ancestors suffered so much from the tyranny of beliefs which reason could not justify, that it was to be expected that they should feel as if errors of the intellect were of all the most deadly, and as if, of all the counsels they could give, " Beware of superstition," was the most important.

Yet if we made this our only rule we might be made uncomfortable when our own beliefs were challenged, and we were called on to show that we were ourselves perfectly free from superstition. I will not dwell on attacks on our faith made by unbelievers, who set down as superstition things which we count part of religion. For example, the one point which Paul felt to be common ground between himself and King Agrippa, when he asked the question, "Believest thou the prophets?" would be challenged by many at the present day who reject the authority of the Jewish prophets, and will not admit that all their predictions came to pass. But I confine myself to cases in which we ourselves might own that beliefs, in which we heartily sympathise, have been carried to faulty excess. What authority do we reverence more than that of the Bible, yet has not that book been sometimes used as a kind of fetish? Has it not been used as a kind of conjuring book? It is on record of a pious clergyman of the last century,[1] a contemporary of John Wesley's, that he felt himself bound to a life of celibacy, because

[1] Mr Berridge's letter to Lady Huntingdon. Works, Appendix, p. 508.

"Before I parted with honest Glascott, I cautioned him much against petticoat snares. No trap so mischievous to the field preacher as wedlock, and it is laid for him at every corner. Matrimony has quite maimed poor Charles, and might have spoiled John and George if a wise master had not graciously sent them a brace of ferrets. Dear George has now got his liberty again, and he will shape well if he is not caught by another tenter-hook."

"Eight or nine years ago, having been grievously tormented with housekeepers, I truly had thoughts of looking out for a Jezebel myself. But it seemed highly needful to ask advice of the Lord, so, falling down on my knees before a table, with a Bible between my hands, I besought the Lord to give me a direction; then, letting the Bible fall open of itself, I fixed my eyes immediately on these words: 'When my son was entered into his wedding chamber, he fell down and died' (2 Esdras x. 1). This frightened me heartily, you may easily think; but Satan, who stood pressing at my elbow, not liking the heavenly caution, presently suggested a scruple that the Book was Apocryphal, and the words not to be heeded. Well, after a short pause, I fell on my knees again, and prayed the Lord not to be angry with me, whilst, like Gideon, I requested a second sign, and from the Canonical Scripture. Then, letting my Bible fall open as before, I fixed my eyes directly on this passage: 'Thou shalt not take thee a wife, neither shalt thou have sons or daughters in this place' (Jer. xvi. 2). I was now completely satisfied, and being thus completely satisfied with my Lord's mind, I make it one part of my prayers. And I can look on these words not only as a rule of direction, but as a promise of security—

practising a mode of ascertaining the divine will
which many other good people had adopted, he shut
his eyes, opened the Bible at random, and put his
finger on the text in Jeremiah, " Thou shalt not take
thee a wife, neither shalt thou have sons or daughters
in this place." And though this kind of sortilege is
not in fashion now, yet is not a chapter of the Bible

' *Thou shalt not take thee a wife,*' that is, I will keep thee from
taking one."

" This method of procuring divine intelligence is much flouted
by flimsy professors who walk at large and desire not that
sweet and secret access to the Mercy Seat that babes of the
Kingdom do find. During the last twelve years I have had
occasion to consult the oracle three or four times on matters
that seemed important and dubious, and have received answers
full and plain. Was not this the practice of the Jewish Church?
God gave laws and statutes to them as well as to us, but when
dubious cases arose they consulted the oracle, which gave
directions how to act. Joshua and Israel are blamed for not
consulting the oracle before they made a league with the
Gibeonites. Yet, in the Patriarchal times we find Rebecca
enquiring of the Lord concerning her twins. And can we
think that God will deny that direction to the Christian
Church that He freely gave to the Jewish? Is not access to
the Mercy Seat more free and more open than before? I
believe these perplexed cases are often sent on purpose to
teach us to enquire of the Lord."

" However, this oracular enquiring is not to be made on light
and trifling occasions, and much less with a light and trifling
spirit. Whoever consults the oracle aright will enter on the
enquiry with the same solemnity as the High Priest entered
into the Holy of Holies, neither must this be done on any day
but a high day, not on trifling occasions, but on very important
concerns. [And he accounts for people not getting relevant
answers to their having asked about trifling matters which
could plainly be resolved by the Word, or only require common
faith and waiting.] God is willing to be consulted, but He
is not willing to be trifled with, and much less to be made the
subject of comment and diversion."

often read as a kind of charm? It matters not from
what book the chapter is taken; it matters not that
the question is never asked, "Understandest thou
what thou readest?" the mere reading is counted the
fulfilment of a religious duty, just as the omission of
prayer would be felt to be shocking by those who are
not shocked at saying the words of prayer while heart
and thoughts are far away. Yet if we had no other
choice than between retaining the faulty excesses
into which reverence for the Bible has led, and
abandoning that reverence, could we hesitate? Are
not our sympathies now with Berridge, in spite of his
Bibliomancy, rather than with Tom Paine and
Voltaire, and the other scoffers of his day?

In like manner we are right in rejecting the
Judaistic formality into which Sabbath observance
was carried in Scotland and in New England, where
it was thought, and still is (though those who think
so are not so numerous as in former days), that to
shave on Sunday, or take a walk for pleasure, or to
whistle a tune, was a sin against Almighty God. We
count it superstitious to be bound by such rules; yet
if we had to choose between their observance and the
making no difference between the Lord's Day and
any other, we could not part with the institution of
hallowing one day in seven, the observance of which
has had so much influence in making our Protestant
countries a God-fearing people.

But if we count as superstition all those unjustified
beliefs which love and reverence suggest, we should
have to own that we have been all from our childhood trained in superstition. In the discipline of a
well-ordered household the child is taught to look on

his parents as the wisest of counsellors, and to feel it his duty implicitly to obey their commands. The truth may be that these parents were but ordinary people, and it may be that in their dealings with their children they were not always wise. Yet one would do the child very ill service who tried to reduce his opinion of his parents to its true scientific value.

A little girl lavishes care and affection on her doll ; makes it the actor in imaginary dramas ; if it is treated with contumely, or if other mishap befalls it, is as much grieved as if a living child were hurt. Should we not think a man a fool who spent his time in trying to convince her of what she knows as well as he, that this work of man's hands is not susceptible of pain or sorrow, when he ought rather to witness with pleasure the early manifestation of those maternal instincts which are afterwards to find more worthy objects of care. Boy and girl grow up. In time she may find some one whom she believes to be wiser, more deserving of trust and confidence than any other man, though perhaps others fail to discover the intellect which she admires in him. He too, may, find some one whom he regards as fairer and more attractive than the rest of her sex. Perhaps his happy experience of wedded life leads him to believe that no other woman is holy, and wise, and good as she. That is not true. Thank God, it is not true, for when she was formed Nature did not break the mould. Many other such there be, and happy is he who finds them. If to hold beliefs, dictated by love and reverence, but which go beyond what reason can justify, be superstition, this man is superstitious, but it is a superstition which is the happiness of his life. In

H

fact, the illusions that spring from love are rarely hurtful, however hateful those may be which are born of coward fear.

Do you suppose, then, that I mean to teach that, provided a belief bring happiness, it matters little whether it be true or false? Far be it from me so to teach. It can never be right, knowingly to cherish a false belief; for out of beliefs arise feelings, from feelings spring actions, and if the beliefs be false there is a risk that the actions will be wrong. Even if a belief seem to us conducive to piety, we must not lie even for God; though certainly, conscious as we are of the weakness of our intellects, we are warned, when we find the fruit to be good, to take heed not to be over hasty in pronouncing the tree to be wholly bad. Above all, since it is not by head knowledge that any one is saved, it is a delusion to think that the one great thing is to free the intellect from errors. However clearly we may see things, however superior our knowledge, we may be in God's sight less worthy than others whose intellect is darkened by superstition, but whose heart and conscience is more honestly set to walk faithfully according to the light they have. With such we may well be patient; for to those whose hearts are so set, God is never slow to grant His Holy Spirit when they seek it, and to teach them to know His ways more perfectly. We have need to be tender in our dealings with them, and, when we seek to bring order into the tangled thicket of true and false conceptions which are apt to grow in each of our limited understandings, to be careful lest in plucking up the tares we root up the wheat with them.

SERMON X

INTERCESSORY PRAYER I

"God is my witness, that without ceasing I make mention of you always in my prayers."—ROMANS i. 9.

"Brethren, pray for us."—1 THESS. v. 25.

IT is proper that on this day on which we commemorate the conversion of St Paul, I should speak about that apostle and his work. But Paul's was a many-sided character, and it would furnish materials for many sermons if I had to speak of all the profitable subjects for study that his life suggests. What I select to speak on now is the importance he attached to intercessory prayer. Almost every one of his Epistles begins as does that to the Romans, one of the opening sentences of which I read to you, by expressing the thankfulness to God which he felt at hearing of the good progress of his disciples and their steadfastness in the faith, and by assuring them of his constant habit of offering prayer on their behalf. And I also read you one sample out of many passages in which he asks his disciples in return to offer their prayers for him.

Ever since, mutual intercessory prayer in public and in private has been the daily practice of the Christian Church. We may regard it as initiated by our Lord Himself, who, in the prayer which He taught His disciples, instructed them to use the plural number, bidding us address God as *Our* Father, asking Him to give *us our* daily bread, to forgive *us our* trespasses. So that even in the solitude of our chambers we do not come to God alone, but bring our brethren with us in our thoughts, and ask blessings for them as well as for ourselves, from their Father and ours.

That instinct which in the hour of anxiety drives all men to prayer has been represented as arising only from the weakness of our nature, as a mad attempt to force all-seeing wisdom into compliance with our weak and erring wills, and it has been said that as we advance in the spiritual life, and as our wills grow into conformity with the Divine will, we shall cease to present requests to God, and be satisfied patiently to wait events in resigned submission to His will. To this it is a sufficient practical answer to say that there was once in the world One who, as even unbelievers must confess, had perpetually before Him the sense of God's presence, and who made the promotion of His glory His rule of life, in a degree which no one has ever equalled, One completely unselfish and absorbed in plans for the good of others. If we think of Him rightly He felt not some of those needs which drive us to prayer : the need of forgiveness of sins, the sense of man's frailty which without the Divine help cannot but fall. And yet His life was pre-eminently a life of prayer, and we read of His spending whole nights in communion with His Father. Thus we learn that when man attains his highest perfection, his greatest conformity to God's will, it is still the need of his nature to pour out his soul before God. And we can understand that just in proportion as any one has a constant sense of the presence of God, as he strives

to do God's will in all things and so to deserve the
title of the friend of God, in that proportion will he
be ready to lay his own wishes before God.   For there
can be no thorough friendship where there is any
restraint such as to prevent either party from communicating his desires to the other.   But he who from
his heart believes in a personal God who condescends
to be called the Friend of men, if he have faith to lay
hold on the high privilege offered him, will delight to
lay bare every wish of his soul to Him who he knows
loves him, and will do more for him than either he
can ask or think.

I have said that speculative objections to prayer
are practically disposed of by our Lord's example.
Now it is to intercessory prayer that that example
most forcibly applies.   If we had been told nothing
on the subject we should have guessed that our Lord's
prayers would be taken up less with petitions for
Himself than requests for the welfare of His people
and aspirations for the glory of His Father.   But we
are not left to conjecture, for in that prayer which St
John has recorded in his seventeenth chapter we are
admitted to the secrets of our Lord's communion with
His Father, and see Him commencing on earth the
work of intercession which He still carries on at the
right hand of God.

And here I must say something as to what Scripture
tells us of our Lord still interceding for us ; of the
Holy Spirit interceding for us :—

> " Not prayer is made on earth alone ;
>   The Holy Spirit pleads,
> And Jesus on the eternal throne
>   For sinners intercedes."

This opens to us new views as to the dignity of prayer. That which we doubted whether it be fitted for really enlightened men turns out not only to become man in his most perfect state but even to be not unworthy of Deity itself.

In fact, the Scripture teaching as to the extent and efficacy of prayer by which man has power with God differs from popular conceptions in the same way that Scripture teaching as to the power of God Himself differs from popular conceptions. Mankind in general are accustomed to think of God as acting only when they see a miracle, or what is to them instead of a miracle, something quite unlike the ordinary course of nature. But with deeper thought we learn that the ordinary operations of nature are to the full as wonderful, and exhibit signs of the Divine working as much, as those which we call miraculous. Take what we account as the most stupendous of all miracles ; it would not manifest God's power more were life to return to animate a dead body, than the same power is daily exhibited in the mysterious process by which inanimate matter becomes capable of life and thought. We are thus led to think of God not as putting forth occasional exercises of power to interfere violently with an established course of nature, which is imagined to proceed at other times independently of Him, but as ever working ; as much in those ordinary acts, which because of the regularity of their succession do not surprise us, as in those which we call miraculous, because the laws which regulate them are unknown to us. And so with regard to prayer. The notion of prayer too common in the world, is that men, habitually forgetful of God, in the time of some

great trouble, fly to prayer in the hope that it will work
some kind of miracle on their behalf. But Scripture
teaches us to look on prayer not as something which
manifests itself occasionally in order to gain for men
something on which their hearts are set, but as the very
breath of the Christian's daily life. It is that communion of the soul with God which—not subjugates
His will to ours, but makes His will ours wherein we
grow more closely united to Him, a communion so
noble that the words which express it can also be
used to express the mysterious intercourse which the
persons of the Godhead have with each other.

But prayer is not merely that which unites the
individual Christian to his God as the source of his
growth in the spiritual life: it is that which binds the
whole Church into one body, each offering supplication for each, each for the whole, the whole for each.
None of them coming to God singly, but all bound
together by mutual intercession. It is indeed wonderful that our privilege of likeness to Christ extends so
far as this that we, unworthy though we are to ask
anything from God, are allowed to take a share in
Christ's work and act as intercessors for our brethren.
And what can train us to likeness to Christ so much
as prayers in which all thought of self being cast
aside we pour out our hearts in manifestation of our
love to our brethren, and in longings for the extension
of the Redeemer's Kingdom in the world. And
surely the higher advances any makes in the spiritual
life, the more he rises above self, the larger space
will requests for others occupy in his devotions.
Now this is a fact of which no satisfactory account
can be given by those philosophic theories current at

the present day, which pretend to explain the efficacy
of prayer without supposing that in it takes place any
real intercourse between the soul and God.   According to these theories prayer for spiritual blessings is
expedient, because prayer is in itself a most powerful
agent for procuring these blessings.   If we desire
meekness to bear reproach, fortitude to bear suffering,
resignation under God's chastening hand, it is admitted
that we can use no more effectual way to obtain these
graces than to pray for them.   But it is imagined
that they come, not by any special interference of
God's Spirit in answer to prayer, but in the way of
natural consequence, our act of prayer having itself
placed our mind in the frame in which we desired it
to be.   Those who hold these views condemn prayer
for temporal blessings, because in this case they can
see no links of natural causation connecting our
prayers with the gaining of the blessings we ask for.
And it is said that if all prayer for temporal blessings
were given up, that kind of prayer whose moral value
is the highest would still remain.

But it is forgotten that intercessory prayer is an
exercise of the very highest moral value, which more
than anything else lifts the soul out of self and ex-
pends it in love to others.   Such prayer for others is
impossible, unless it can be accompanied by belief
that it will benefit those on whose behalf it is offered.
No one could be guilty of the hypocrisy of praying for
others solely in order to do good to himself.   And
yet it is evident that in the way of natural consequence prayer can benefit none but him who offers it.
It follows then that any theory which does not recognize prayer as direct intercourse with a personal

God, who is able and willing to answer the petitions made Him, is unable to give any rational justification of that class of prayer the practice of which is of the highest moral value in elevating the character of the worshipper. Believe in a God at all, and you can have no hesitation in choosing between the two theories of prayer. The one theory is that it is a kind of self-mesmerism, the practice of which is of the greatest possible advantage, but which becomes more and more difficult as the worshipper becomes more enlightened, so that in the end he refuses to permit the instincts of his nature to deceive him, even though forced to acknowledge that the deceit would be for his good. Who can help preferring the Christian theory of prayer, namely, that the Author of our nature who has so constituted us that the practice of prayer is our best safeguard against temptation, and our best comfort in sorrow, has provided that the grounds of this practice shall have objective reality, and that the idea that in prayer we can have present intercourse with an all-powerful Friend is not a happy self-deception but a blessed truth. In particular, prayer for others finds its only justification if prayer be not a communing of our own thoughts with themselves, but an address to One who Himself loves those for whom we pray, and who has Himself commanded us to ask on their behalf.

Our Lord, at any rate, has decided that question for us. He has not only instructed us to pray for each other, but He has given special promises to united prayer, to the prayers offered by His Church. Not necessarily in any very large assembly. He has said, "If two or three of you shall agree in anything you ask, it shall be done for you by My Father which is in Heaven." " Wheresoever two or three are gathered together in My name, there am I in the midst of you." And from the time He taught these lessons, in every assembly of Christians from the very earliest times, according to the apostles' command, prayers and supplications, intercessions and giving of thanks have been wont to be made for all men. The comprehensive petitions of our Litany in which every class of men, who, by any possibility, can be supposed to need our prayers is successively prayed for, are framed after models of the most venerable antiquity. And from the very first the most solemn act of Christian worship was never limited to seeking the benefits of those actually present, but was made to include intercession for the whole state of Christ's Church.

Natural religion might teach men the relation which each individually held towards his Creator ; it might teach them that He who had made them watched over His creatures, would punish their misconduct, was pleased with their obedience, and was willing to accept their worship. But our Lord added to this a doctrine which was felt to be so novel and important that from very early times it has been included in that short summary of cardinal verities in which every Christian testifies his belief ; each of whom makes his profession, I believe in the Communion of Saints. Religion, according to our Lord's teaching, does not consist in the solitary exercise of devout aspirations of the soul after God, but He has formed His disciples into one body, of which He is the head, from which all the body, by joints and bands, having nourishment ministered, and knit together, increases with the increase of God. As each separate member has no independent life, but perishes if cut off from that nourishment which is diffused from the head through the body, so each member sympathizes with all the rest. Whether one member suffer, all the members suffer with it, or one member be honoured, all the members rejoice with it; and the consequence of this union of Christ's people into one body is that the wants of each individual are wants of the whole, and so when Christians assemble for united prayer, they join in supplication that God will supply the needs of each member according to his several necessity. And conversely the wants of the whole are wants of each individual, and so each Christian in his private devotion will, if he be truly a living member of the body, not think merely of his own individual necessities, but earnestly pray also for the welfare of the whole, and as far as his knowledge of the wants of others extends, supplicate that God will supply their needs according to the riches of His grace.

It is hard to include in one sermon all that is necessary for a full discussion of the subject of intercessory prayer. Many questions have been raised about it. For instance, it has been asked, How far does this Communion of Saints of which I have spoken extend? Does it not include those already departed out of the body as well as those still militant here on earth? Ought we not to believe that departed saints pray for us, and would it not be wise to ask their prayers? And ought not we to pray for them? I will not attempt to answer any such questions now, but I hope this afternoon to resume the discussion of the subject.

SERMON XI

INTERCESSORY PRAYER II

"God is my witness, that without ceasing I make mention of you always in my prayers."—ROMANS i. 9.

"Brethren, pray for us."—1 THESS. v. 25.

I RETURN now to consider some questions concerning intercessory prayer that there was not time to discuss this morning. There are some cautions that need to be given both to those that offer prayer for others, and to those who desire that others should pray for them. No religion has inspired such self-sacrificing love for others as Christianity; yet some of its doctrines, if they stood alone, would have stimulated in the highest degree the selfish part of our nature. I refer to its revelation that on the use we make of our time of probation here, depends our happiness, not only in this life, but throughout eternity. And it is true, that there are those who have made their religion only a scheme for getting as much happiness for themselves as they can in both worlds. When they find that it is not enough selfishly to scheme for their prosperity here, they aim at arranging that they shall be prosperous in the next world too. The terrors of Divine Justice led many to feel that the one great object for any man to set himself was how to save his own soul. "What shall it profit a man," asked our Lord, "if he gain the whole world, and lose his own soul?" They went further, and asked, What shall it profit me if the whole world be saved and not I? Many then fled to deserts, and abandoning all attempts to benefit their fellow-creatures, hoped, by solitary devotions and austerities, at least to secure their own salvation.

When such conduct is stigmatised as selfish, there is an answer ready: viz., if these men did not work for their fellow-creatures, at least they prayed for them, and since God is stronger than men, doubtless the prayers of saints like these did their brethren more good than they could have effected by any exertion of their own. But God who works in us does not choose to work without us. If we work and pray, our work receives a blessing; if we pray without working, our prayer is but hypocrisy. St James has asked: "If a brother or sister be naked and destitute of daily food, and one of you say to them, Depart in peace, be ye warmed and filled, notwithstanding ye give them not those things which are needful to the body, what doth it profit?" A satirist has said that the instinct of compassion is so deeply planted in the human heart, that no one can see a fellow-creature in distress without wishing that some one else should relieve him. Yet our intercessions with other people for that purpose would not have much chance of success, if we begged for charities to which we refused to subscribe a penny of our own money. And can we suppose that we are at liberty to deal with God in a manner in which it would be unworthy to deal with our fellow-creatures?

Surely every intercession we offer to God implies an obligation on ourselves. So our Lord has expressly taught us in one case. When we say not, "forgive *me* my trespasses," but "forgive *us* our trespasses," He bids us ask ourselves, Well, if besides offences against God, there are offences against ourselves, do *we* forgive? But the same principle runs through every petition of our Lord's prayer, testing whether or not we are sincere in uttering it. When we say, "Thy Kingdom come," we must ask, are we doing anything to make it come? When we say, "Thy will be done in earth as it is in Heaven," are we striving to do that will ourselves? are we striving to influence others to do it? When we say not, "give *me my* daily bread," but "give *us our* daily bread," what do we give ourselves? do we help to supply daily bread to those who want it? One of my early recollections is hearing a charity sermon from one of the most popular charity-sermon preachers of the day, Ludlow Tonson, who was afterwards Bishop of Killaloe. He commented on what was then an ordinary form of grace after meat: "Lord, relieve the wants of others, and make us thankful for all Thy mercies." That is to say, you thank God for all He has done for yourselves; and as for others, well, you hope God will take care of them too. "Nay," he cried, "you ought not to say, 'Lord, relieve the wants of others,' but, 'Lord, teach *us* to relieve the wants of others.'" And those who tendered prayer for others as a substitute for active exertions on their behalf, had no right to expect that such a substitute would either be effectual or be accepted.

It remains to give a caution as to asking the prayers

of others. There is an important distinction between intercession and mediation. Each ought to intercede, and does intercede, for the rest, but we have but one Mediator between God and men—the Man Christ Jesus. There is a feeling which sometimes leads men to ask the prayers of others—a feeling that they themselves are not good enough to be worthy to address God, but that He will be more likely to listen to other men who are supposed to have higher claims on His favour.[1] It was this feeling which seems to have prompted Simon Magus to ask for the apostle's prayers. When St Peter warned him, "Pray God if perhaps the thought of thine heart may be forgiven thee, for I perceive that thou art in the gall of bitterness and the bond of iniquity," Simon, conscious that the apostle's estimate of his character was correct, and, feeling his unfitness to pray, answers : ' Pray ye to the Lord for me, that none of these things which ye have spoken come upon me." To ask for the prayers of others from such motives as this, is to send others to God instead of us, while we ourselves remain away : it is making them mediators between us and God, and intercepting some of the regards which we owe to the great Answerer of prayer. But, though we are taught in the Gospel that man for his manifold sins is unworthy to ask anything of God in his own name, it teaches also that we who were some-time afar off are brought nigh by the blood of Christ, and are privileged to ask in His name. Our only Mediator has removed every obstacle between us and God, and if our consciousness of sin makes us afraid to approach Him, we have but to think of that

[1] *See* Terence, "Adelphi," IV. v. 70.

wonderful parable of the prodigal son : " When he was yet a great way off, his father saw him, and had compassion on him, and ran and fell on his neck and kissed him." When we think of that affecting picture of our Father's willingness to receive back His repentant wanderers, each of us can feel, I, too, am a son. Through my Saviour, Jesus, I am privileged to come boldly to my Father's presence. I have many brothers who have not trangressed His commands as I have done, yet I, no less than they, am the object of His boundless love, and may come near Him without fear of repulse.

When, as in the text and elsewhere, St Paul asks for the prayers of his disciples, it surely was not that they were better entitled to God's favour, or more likely to be heard, than he. If our right to pray for others depended on their being less worthy than ourselves, it would have been very presumptuous in Paul's converts if they had taken him at his word, and given him the prayers for which in mistaken humility he asked. And further, as each Christian advanced in Christian humility, and in lowliness of mind esteemed others better than himself, he would hesitate to pray for others, and, shrinking from coming to God himself, would ask them to intercede on his behalf. But the true theory of Christian intercession does not for a moment disturb our faith in God's infinite willingness to answer the prayers of the humblest of His people. We have special commands and special promises to mutual prayer, and we can well believe that the united prayers of Paul's converts on his behalf were effectual in obtaining for that apostle from God a still larger measure of His Holy Spirit. Mutual prayer of this kind does not keep any one at a distance from God, but, on the contrary, brings all nearer. And nothing can better enable us to realise the Communion of Saints, nothing can more thoroughly make us feel that we are one body, than if, instead of each striving singly to secure his own salvation, we strive one for another, not only helping each other by counsel and active exertions, but also striving for one another in mutual supplications at the Mercy Seat of the Most High.

There remains something which I promised to say on the question, How far does the Communion of Saints, of which I have spoken, extend? Out of difference of opinion on this subject has arisen considerable difference in the practical usages of professing Christians. We all agree that the Church which our senses disclose to us, militant here in earth, is not the whole of the Church. Those whom death has taken from the world do not cease to exist. They have been merely removed out of our sight. Now it is urged that as friends separated on earth may be still united at the Throne of Grace, so a similar communion of mutual intercessions may take place between the Church on earth and that in the unseen world, they praying for us and we for them.

Now Scripture is very silent as to the state of the departed, and we are left to form our own conjectures. That the departed continue to love those whom they had loved on earth, and to show their love by praying for them, is so probable that we may well believe it. That they have knowledge of what takes place on earth after their deaths is a point on which we have no information at all. These are merely speculative questions, but they lead up to the practical question,

I

Shall we do well to ask them for their prayers?
There is no rational ground for believing that they
can hear the requests made to them by those who
ask their intercession; still less, that they have such
virtual omnipresence as to be able to hear simultaneously requests addressed to them from a multitude of different places. Now the silence of Scripture
amounts to a very strong argument; for though the
Bible is habitually silent about merely speculative
questions, it never is silent about anything that
concerns our practice, and if it would benefit us
to ask the prayers of the departed, we may be sure
that it would have given us some command or some
encouragement to do so. There is no precept and
no example. I have often thought it remarkable
that St Paul, who so often speaks of the mercy
showed to him who had once persecuted the Church
of God, never ascribes that mercy to the intercession
of St Stephen, although that martyr died in an
act of prayer for Paul and his other murderers.
Scripture in another way discourages us from seeking
the intercession of the departed, namely, by the
prominence which it gives to the intercession of
Jesus, of whose power to help us, and of whose
loving willingness to hear us, we can have no doubt.
It was three or four centuries before requests for
saintly intercession came into use in the Church, and
our own Church acccordingly gives no sanction to
them.

   And what I said just now about the difference
between mediation and intercession will explain how
seeking the intercession of departed saints may be
mischievous in a way that asking for the prayers of a

living person never can be. Though we may believe other men to be far more holy than ourselves, still our confidence in them must always be mixed up with enough of doubt to prevent our trust in their prayers from superseding the necessity for our own. But no such distrustful feelings are entertained respecting the Blessed Virgin and the saints. They who are sure of such prayers really need not to come to God directly, and if they offer their prayers to Him, they do so rather as an honour which it is their duty to pay Him, than as a privilege needful to them for their own sakes. Thus the saints have come to be regarded as a kind of inferior divinities likely to be more indulgent to human frailties than the Supreme God. If there be any being whose intercession with God is supposed to be of unbounded efficacy, that being practically becomes a god to us. For if we need help in time of need it makes no practical difference how he to whom we turn for help comes to possess his power to help us ; whether it arises from his own inherent strength, or derived through some one else, provided only we can rely on it as unfailing. That being whom we consider as of unbounded compassion, ready to lend a gracious ear to our petitions, and able to obtain for us the fulfilment of our requests—that being is in truth our god. Now there is no more powerful agent in moral discipline than prayer to the Supreme God, which makes the soul holier and happier by bringing it to delight itself in the felt presence of a Being of infinite purity and infinite love. But the inter-position of others between Him and us has what the prophet long since pointed out as the distinguishing mark of false religion—to make the heart of the righteous sad, and to strengthen the hands of the wicked by promising him life. It saddens the righteous whom it teaches to distrust our Lord, and to doubt His readiness to receive them if they come to Him directly, and it emboldens the wicked by leading them to believe that there are others more merciful than Christ, and who will forgive sins on easier terms than He.

I will only touch briefly on the remaining question, whether in the communion of saints it is not necessary that those on earth should offer prayers for their departed friends. If it is true in general with respect to our prayers that not only because of our unworthiness we dare not, but because of our blindness we know not what to ask, still more is this true with respect to the unseen world, concerning which we are almost altogether ignorant. I think, that if our Lord or His apostles had wished that such prayers should be offered, they would have told us more. Nevertheless, since the apostle has taught us, *In everything* by prayer and supplication, with thanksgiving, let your requests be made known unto God, we need not doubt that whatever anxieties we may entertain, whatever longing desires we have for the happiness of loved ones who have left this earth, all may fitly be entrusted to that sympathising Friend from whom none of our thoughts need be kept back, and who, according to His wisdom, will fulfil our desires in the best way.

I am not disposed to put on the words, " In everything," which I have quoted, any arbitrary restrictions, which would oblige us to regard some of the anxieties that fill our minds as unfit to be made known to our Father in Heaven. For there is no objection that has been raised against the propriety of prayer for others that does not apply with equal force against prayer for ourselves.

For example, it is true that a deeper knowledge of the Saviour's love would release us from the racking anxieties that have often prompted prayers for departed friends. When we learn to know His love, we learn to trust Him, to trust Him not only for ourselves but for those dear to us, being persuaded that our Father Himself loves them and needs no urging to bless them. Yet if the conclusion is drawn that therefore we ought not to offer such prayers, we are bound to remember that the same argument has been used to dissuade us from offering prayers of any kind to one whom we believe to be both all-good and all-wise. He loves us : He knows better than we what things we really have need of : He would, without being asked, grant us all that He saw it to be good that we should have ; why then strive to bring omnipotence to compliance with our erring wills ? Yet speculative difficulties have no force in opposition to the impulses of the nature with which our Creator has endowed us. In time of trouble men fly to God, who have little thought of Him before, while they who have always striven to realize His presence find it an unspeakable privilege to pour out their hearts before Him ; and in this sacred communion gain cheerful hope while the event of their petitions is uncertain, and strength for trustful submission if these petitions should be denied.

Again, what most of all has seemed to conflict with prayers for the departed, is the belief that when a man's earthly life is finished his condition can receive no further change, and that his subsequent destiny so inevitably results from the condition in which he has left this world that to ask for a change is as absurd as to pray for the suspension of a law of nature. I need not enquire whether and how far this assumption is justified, because the objection founded on it, is one with which we must deal if we are to defend prayer of any kind. It was urged by one school of objectors, on theological grounds, that the actual course of events had been fixed long since by the Divine foreknowledge, and now cannot be otherwise than as He had foreseen it : and again by another school on physical grounds, that every change in the material world is the inevitable result of the immediately previous condition through the action of the forces then in operation, so that no place is left in the chain of causation for the work of any incorporeal agent. Plainly, if this argument be pushed, it annihilates not only prayer but all human planning and contriving. We are forced then to ask, Is there any of our actions which is not foreseen by God, or any which is not the result of the action of physical forces which we did not ourselves create?

What is most important to observe is that it is only human limitations that make prayer possible. To God, future and past are equally plain. If we could see as He does, there would be no uncertainty, and therefore no anxiety, no need for prayer. It is because of the limitations of time to which we are subject, that our ignorance of the future fills us with care and anxiety. If God permits us to make known to Him our anxieties in prayer, the boundaries of the province of prayer are determined not by God's knowledge but by our ignorance ; and prayer has its justification, whenever the darkness that clouds our path fills us with cares, all of which He has encouraged us to commit to Him.

Far be it from me then to say that prayer for the dead is wrong. If it were a sin, it is one which it is almost impossible not to commit when we lose one whose name it had been our constant habit to mention in our prayers. In spite of theory, the loved name will still rise to our lips, and then are we bound to suppress our yearnings of desire, or blush that they should be known to our Father who is in Heaven ? In some such way prayers for the dead arose in the early Church. When leading men died, whose names had been habitually mentioned in the public prayers of the Church, to discontinue the mention seeemed inconsistent with the belief that they were not extinct, but still living with Christ. But the sequel of the history seems to indicate that there is danger of founding unauthorised action on speculations of our own, for as a historical fact the use of such prayers led to a great weakening of the sense which Christians felt of the love of God. The first prayers for the dead were the inarticulate cry of a bleeding heart pleading for a blessing from God, without knowing in what form it was to be given, or why it was needed. When such prayers became mere tradition of the past, men began to theorise as to the purposes they were to serve ; theories about torments to be suffered after death by those who had died in the Lord, which torments might be alleviated by mercenary prayers purchased by the bequests of terrified invalids, or by the gifts of their sorrowing friends. And the result was that the abuses came to be so great, that we cannot doubt that our Reformed Church did wisely in removing prayers for the dead from her public offices.

Having said so much about theories of prayer, I will add in conclusion a word as to the practice of it. When it was attempted to perplex one of old with what purported to be a demonstration that motion was impossible, he thought it refutation enough to walk across the room. If any difficulty be raised as to the theory of prayer, your best refutation will be to try it and prove its efficacy. Pray, then, that that Holy Spirit, by whose gift alone you can pray as you ought to pray, may give life and spirit to those desires which now may be cold and feeble, that so you with the rest of Christ's people may, according to His own prayer, form one body closely bound to each other in mutual love, testified by mutual prayer.

SERMON XII

THE TEMPTATION IN THE WILDERNESS

"Then Peter took Him, and began to rebuke Him, saying, Be it far from Thee, Lord : this shall not be unto Thee. But He turned, and said unto Peter, Get thee behind Me, Satan : thou art an offence unto Me : for thou savourest not the things that be of God, but those that be of men.—MATT. xvi. 22, 23.

HAS it ever happened to you that a great approaching calamity has cast its black shadow over your path ? Suppose, for example, that a loved member of your family has been attacked by dangerous illness, and that from all you can learn, the symptoms give little hope of a favourable issue. Has it happened to you in such circumstances to look for sympathy from friends, and to be met with cheering exhortations not to anticipate evil, not to exaggerate the danger which they assure you is nothing like what you had imagined it to be. Such comforting assurances are often easily given because they cost so little. They relieve him who makes them from the burden of a painful demand on him for sympathy. One is not always in a mood to mourn with those who mourn, or even to seem to mourn, and so it is pleasant to be able to persuade oneself that the need for such an effort has not arisen and may never arise. Yet what more chilling than to come looking for sympathy, and receive nothing but the empty husks of flattering assurances which inspire no confidence, because manifestly springing from no real knowledge. It is disheartening to discover that your friends do not love you well enough to care to enter into your anxieties and griefs, but will selfishly refuse to allow danger threatening you to stir them from the easy quiet of their own untroubled lives.

In the case of our Lord's disciples, there is no reason to think that it was want of love for their Master that made them treat His predictions of coming suffering as vain apprehensions. They had had two lessons to learn, and it was just because they had in some measure learned the first that they found it hard to receive another which seemed to them inconsistent with it. What a difficult lesson that first one had been. They had shared in the general expectation of their countrymen that the prophetic announcements of a coming ruler and deliverer of their nation were approaching fulfilment. They had hoped to see a son of David, a king who should rule in righteousness, who should make Jerusalem the joy of the whole earth. It had been no easy task to persuade themselves to recognize this royal hero in a man of lowly rank like themselves, the carpenter's son, whom they had known as kind and good, whom they might have respected as a wise teacher, but who was a man of peace, and seemed no likely person to free the nation from a foreign yoke. If we had not the Gospel account of miracles wrought by our Lord, a sagacious critic might have inferred that something of the kind must have taken place. For how else was it possible that this provincial Rabbi should be greeted in the streets of Jerusalem with cries of Hosanna to the Son of David. It was the mighty works that He performed, which did what nothing else could have done, namely, impress the minds of those about Him with the belief, that here was one possessed of supernatural power sufficient to give success to any cause that He might be induced to lead. You will remember that the effect of one of His miracles, that of feeding the five thousand, was that the multitudes whom He had fed, wanted to take Him by force and make Him a King. Long before this miracle the disciples who were in constant attendance on Him had had frequent occasions to cry, "What manner of man is this?" Our Lord, as we are told in the verses that immediately precede the text, forced them to reflect on what they knew, by asking them, "Whom do men say that I am? Whom say ye that I am?" and though Peter, with his usual promptitude, was the first to give the answer, the answer was one that must have been in the minds of them all, "Thou art the Christ, the Son of the living God."

Now to recognise in Jesus the Messiah, meant something more than to confer on Him a barren title. It meant the belief that He would do all that it had been predicted the Messiah was to do; it meant that He was to be a Sovereign, a victor over the nation's enemies: all kings should fall down before Him, all peoples should do Him service. And with belief in greatness of position for Him, naturally arose ambitious dreams of greatness for themselves. They were His chosen companions : surely they would hold the first places in His kingdom. That they should be great, they did not doubt ; the only question in their minds was, which of the twelve should be the greatest. Two of them, we are told, besought our Lord, or at least supplication was made on their behalf, that they should sit, the one on His right hand, the other on His left hand in His Kingdom. And the anger that this request raised among the disciples against the two brethren, showed what rival claims for the highest place existed. Imagine then the state of feeling which took its rise from the acceptance of the first lesson the disciples had to learn, namely, belief in their Master's Messiahship, and you can judge how incredible the second announcement must have seemed that He must go to Jerusalem and suffer many things of the elders and chief priests and scribes, and be killed.

When a friend seems to us in needlessly low spirits about his own health or the health of members of his family, it is not that we think it impossible that he or they should die. In fact we know they must some day or another, though we prefer to think the event not likely soon to occur. But what Jesus now announced, His disciples believed could *never* occur. How was the Messiah to be King if He was not accepted by the rulers of the people? How was He to reign over other nations if He was not accepted by His own? How was He to reign at all if He was to be killed? Must they banish from their minds as a fond delusion all that they had regarded themselves as authorized to believe of greatness for Him and high place for themselves. The cry, " Be it far from Thee, Lord, this shall not happen to Thee," did not proceed from want of love to Him or from want of interest in His prosperity : it came from the ardour of their love to Him : from the fulness of their belief that it was He to whom the promise had been made, " The enemy shall not do Him violence nor the son of wickedness afflict Him. And I will beat down His adversaries before Him, and smite them that hate Him."

Yet however excusable might be the disciples' inability to sympathize with their Master, not the less do we feel how intense His loneliness must have been when those who loved Him best were so utterly unable to sympathize with Him. On any question concerning our Lord's human nature, we must speak with a certain reserve ; for we need not hesitate to confess that confident speculators have overrated the powers of the human intellect when they have thought themselves able to solve the problem of accurately defining how, when the Divine and human natures were united in one person, the attributes of each nature were affected. Yet we undoubtingly believe that our blessed Lord was perfect Man as well as perfect God ; perfect Man as well in soul as in body ; and that not only did His body need those things by which the human body is refreshed, food and rest ; so that in the absence of them He felt hunger and weariness ; but that His soul also desired those things by which our souls are refreshed, such as the love and sympathy of friends. Yet how little of them He had. Love no doubt in some degree, yet even that failing when it was most needed, as for example when His disciples were asked to watch with Him one hour, or as when hands were laid on Him they all forsook Him and fled, and the boldest of them denied that he had known Him. But for sympathy, He was too much above those who surrounded Him to be able to receive much genuine sympathy from them. I need not now speak of His divine character. The same grief of want of sympathy has had to be borne by all who have enlarged the bounds of human knowledge. Things which they have clearly perceived, or by their genius have divined, have been so far out of the sight of their contemporaries, that their report has been scoffed at as a vain imagination. Such for example were the jeers that Columbus encountered when he propounded at Salamanca his project of a voyage to the unexplored West, and the opposition he met when he prevailed on a reluctant crew to bring his conception to a successful result. Had our Lord been inspired only by human sagacity, He must have had to do most of His work alone; still more so when His divine foreknowledge revealed to Him what toil and suffering must intervene before the victory could be won which His sanguine disciples imagined to be immediate. Thus, when His spirit was in heaviness in the knowledge of the approaching conflict with the powers of darkness, He had to bear His sorrows alone; which were only aggravated by the light-hearted assurances of ignorant and unsympathizing followers: " Be it far from Thee, Lord, this shall not happen unto Thee."

But the words, " Get thee behind Me, Satan," reveal

that our Lord regarded His apostle not merely as
withholding the help and comfort he might have
been expected to afford, but actually as taking part
with His adversary. I suppose there is no subject
in dealing with which we are bound to walk more
warily than when we speak of our Lord as in His
human nature subject to temptation; but as to the
fact that He was so subject we can be certain; for
that He was so tempted is recorded in what even an
unbeliever ought to acknowledge to be one of the
most authentic portions of the Gospel history. This
story of the temptation is one most unlikely to have
been imagined by a disciple, as we well know from
the difficulty every Christian feels in thinking it to be
possible that one who was without spot of sin could
be tempted like as we are. A Christian philosopher
has showed that a completely sinless being may be
subject to temptation; our desires and appetites are
in themselves perfectly innocent, and though there
may be occasions when we cannot rightly gratify
them, yet not the less will they be felt, and to refuse
them gratification must involve a struggle. Thus
that our Lord when He had fasted should afterwards
have hungered is consistent with the most perfect
sinlessness, and equally so that He should have
desired to appease that hunger when He had the
power to do so. If higher reasons forbade the gratification of that desire there must have ensued that
conflict between opposing parts of man's nature to
which we give the name of temptation. But though
there is nothing to which we need refuse belief in
the Gospel story of our Lord's temptation; yet we
can safely say that it was one most unlikely to be

invented by attached and revering followers to whose feelings it must have been as repugnant as it is to our own to think of Him as liable to any of the weaknesses of humanity, or as capable even of a wish to do anything forbidden by the highest law. The story, if not invented by His disciples, must have been communicated by their Master Himself to those on whose testimony it was recorded. And when we examine the narrative we can be assured that this was so, for the character of the temptations described is such that it is next to impossible that they could have been imagined by one who had not actually experienced them. None of them belongs to the class of temptations which ordinary men experience or which imagination would suggest to the inventor of a fictitious story. They all turn on the case of a man conscious of the possession of supernatural power and free to exercise it as he will, and the problem is, what limitations would a perfect man put on the exercise of his power. That is a problem which none but one had ever to determine for Himself.

The first temptation was to exercise supernatural power for the relief of His own wants. Not only did that present itself in the wilderness when it was suggested to Him that He should command stones to be made bread; but afterwards when He went about, not knowing where to lay His head, and supported by the ministrations of faithful women. There was a shorter method of supplying His wants, if He were to use for His own needs that power which He so often applied for the relief of others. The temptation to cast Himself down from the pinnacle of the temple was the same as that which He afterwards resisted when asked to show a sign from Heaven; namely, so to use His supernatural power as to compel all the people to immediate acknowledgment of His claims. And the offer that the prince of this world should yield Him peaceable possession of all his kingdoms was a temptation which in various forms presented itself again; the offer to yield Him the palm of victory without the dust of conflict; to make Him to escape the sorrows of Gethsemane, the jeers and buffets of the judgment hall, the Cross of Calvary, desertion by His disciples, rejection by those He came to save, and thus to mount, without a contest, the throne of David. Such for example might be His lot if He consented to those who were eager to make Him a King, and if putting Himself at their head He used His supernatural power to destroy His enemies.

I have said that the story of our Lord's temptation was one most unlikely to have been invented by disciples who would find it difficult to think of Him as tempted at all, and, in any case, would never have dreamed of such temptations as those recorded in the Gospels. But, on the other hand, if this had been a real experience of His own, were there not many occasions when it would be natural that He should tell His disciples of it. That which, in speaking of Him, we call a temptation, must to the disciples have been a perplexing difficulty: why should their Master have nothing, if in truth He possessed all things? Why should His ministers suffer poverty and contempt if they were indeed heirs of a glory hereafter to be revealed? Was there not need that these murmurers should be told how Satan had offered

Himself an easier lot, and that He had refused to accept the boon at his hands; so that they could be but ministers of Satan, if they pressed on Him the proposal which the Evil One had made Him at the very beginning of His work.

That He had thus actually told the story may reasonably be inferred from the language of His rebuke to Peter, "Get thee behind Me, Satan." It is not conceivable that He would use words so harsh to a faithful and attached disciple, if He had given him no clue to the meaning of them. But admit that Jesus had previously told the story of the temptation, and we see that His quotation of the very words in which He had before rebuked Satan himself, could need no comment to make Peter understand what part he was now playing.

St Luke finishes his account of the temptation in the wilderness by saying that the tempter departed from Him for a season. We have seen that there were more occasions than one when the temptation was renewed; in particular at Gethsemane, when His human nature shrank from anticipation of the agony that was impending, and He besought, that if it were possible, the cup might pass from Him. Suppose that one of ourselves had undertaken at the call of duty a difficult and dangerous task. Suppose for instance that a man had resolved to enter a burning house in order to save the life of some one within; and suppose all the bystanders were to cry out to him to turn back; that the thing was impossible, that he was sacrificing his life uselessly, how all this would tend to shake his resolution and unnerve his courage.

Now, our Lord, as man, was alive to all the

influences of human sympathy, and therefore it must have added to His sufferings, that those who ought to have been His support did their best to dissuade Him and keep Him back from His work. In this case His chief and chosen apostle rejected the ideas of failure and death as in His case a degrading and inadmissible conception; and played the part of the tempter more effectually because in the guise of an attached friend.

What a transformation we have in the course of a few verses : the same man addressed by his Master, with, " Blessed art thou"; hailed as honoured by a special revelation from God the Father ; named as the rock on which Christ's Church was to be built, and promised the keys of the Kingdom of Heaven : and shortly afterwards reprobated as a Satan laying a stone of stumbling in his Lord's way. Surely we must say, " Let him that thinketh he standeth take heed lest he fall." Deceitful often is the self-confidence that springs out of a real success. He who has not deceived himself in thinking that he has been able, deeper than others, to sound the mysteries of God, is tempted to imagine his plummet has reached the bottom, and to think too highly of his superficial knowledge. He combines the truths of which he is assured, and ventures to draw inferences from them; yet of what inference can we be more sure than Peter felt himself to be when he judged that it was not possible that the Christ, the Son of the living God, could be even for a moment overcome by death.

If Peter had imagined himself to have been con-stituted by our Lord, as in later times it has been fancied he was, the ruler and guide of the apostles, they would have been led under his guidance into the miserable error of preferring such temporal glory as Satan claimed to be able to offer, the honours and riches of this world, to that victory over the powers of darkness which through suffering and death Christ won on the Cross, even eternal life for those that believe on Him.

SERMON XIII

THE RESPONSIBILITIES OF PRIVILEGE

" Ye are the salt of the earth : but if the salt have lost his savour, wherewith shall it be salted? it is thenceforth good for nothing, but to be cast out, and to be trodden under foot of men."

—MATT. v. 13.

MOST of you will remember that these words are part of the first recorded discourse of our Lord, which we commonly know as the Sermon on the Mount. This title reminds us not only of the place where the discourse was delivered, but also of the audience to which it was addressed. St Matthew had told at the end of the preceding chapter of the crowds who had been collected by the fame of our Lord's miracles, and who, as another evangelist tells us, thronged Him, so that He had scarce time to take food. These He taught by the shores of the Lake, and after the call of Peter, He was able by getting into Peter's boat to relieve Himself of the pressure. But at this early stage He escaped the crowd by going inland and ascending the mountain above Capernaum. There He was followed only by those who were called His disciples, from among whom He chose those whom He afterwards called apostles ; and it was to these disciples that the Sermon on the Mount was addressed.

149

If this did not appear from the historical narrative, it could be inferred from the topics of the discourse. The words, " Ye are the light of the world," " Ye are the salt of the earth," were not addressed to the motley crowd of unthinking sight-seers whom curiosity had gathered round Him. He tells His disciples first of their privileges, then of the responsibility which these privileges bring.

He begins by telling them of the blessedness of those who cast in their lot with Him. He does not disguise from them, that in joining Him they must bid farewell to the riches and honours of this world. Yet, " Blessed are ye poor, for yours is the Kingdom of Heaven. Blessed are ye that hunger and thirst after righteousness : for ye shall be filled. Blessed are ye when men shall revile you, and persecute you, and say all manner of evil against you falsely, for My sake. Rejoice in that day and be exceeding glad, for great is your reward in Heaven."

What immediately follows the Beatitudes was clearly addressed to the disciples. It was not to the ordinary mixed multitude that He said, "Ye are the light of the world." It was to those whom He was educating to spread through the world the truths which He was teaching them. But to them He went on to show that privileges bring responsibility. The knowledge He bestowed on them was not for their personal delectation. The light that He communicated was not to be hidden under the bushel. It was set up, in order that it might give light to the whole house. This is true of all who learn anything from Him, but it was specially true of those whom He meant to employ as teachers. These words, " Ye are the light of the

world," may perhaps be supposed to refer mainly to
intellectual enlightenment, but those which immediately follow, "Ye are the salt of the earth," plainly
refer to moral influence; and both were true, not of
the motley crowd of curious seekers for excitement,
but of the little society which our Lord was then
forming.

And was it not true that founded as that society
was, which we now know under the name of the
Christian Church, in a time of immense and continually growing moral corruption, this society, more
than any other influence, stayed the evil, preserved
and restored those principles of truth and purity
which God had written in the hearts of men, but
which human passions had infected; and gave back
their rightful supremacy to conscience and law. It
is hard to overrate the influence exercised by a body
of men whose conduct is habitually ruled by these
principles, even on those who do not theoretically
own them; for there is in each man's heart a silent
witness to their truth. And certain it is that from
the time of the preaching of Christianity we find a
constant rising of the moral tone even of heathen
writers. But here, too, the announcement of privilege
is accompanied by a warning. If the salt have lost
its savour, it is thenceforth good for nothing but to be
cast out and trodden under the foot of men. It was
with a view to speak of this warning that I chose
my text. We do not much need to be reminded of
our privileges, but we do need to be warned of our
dangers, and my reading of the history of the world
is, that there is no danger which we are more apt to
overlook than the tendency of salt to lose its savour—

that is to say, speaking without any metaphor, the fact that institutions and doctrines, the inculcation of which have conferred the greatest benefit on their generation, are apt, as time goes on, to lose their salutary power, and thus, we must admit, often deservedly lose the estimation in which they had been held.

I need take no better example than that religion of the Jews, which, for thousands of years but of local influence, has now spread over all the world, and notwithstanding separation both in time and place, rules at the present day the lives of us in these distant isles. The Jews may be said to have been the light of the world. If it owes its knowledge of art to Athens and of law to Rome, it is indebted to Jerusalem for religion. While other nations worshipped gods many and lords many, long before science had taught the unity of all the physical forces of the universe, the Jews recognised a single Supreme Sovereign Ruler of all. Yet they are open to the reproach of having hid their light. They cared to make no proselytes. Perhaps it was wisely so arranged. Probably the result of too free intercourse with other nations more numerous and more powerful would have been that, instead of illuminating others, their own light would have been darkened. At all events, if this jealous warding off of unfriendly blasts preserved their own light unextinguished, it shut out for centuries the rest of the world from profiting by it. And they were also the salt of the earth. Their code of morals, for which they claimed greater antiquity than was possessed by any heathen legislation, also excelled every other in purity. Men are apt to imagine their deity to be like themselves, but in no case will they deny to the beings whom they adore, excellences which they themselves aspire to. You cannot expect people to be better than the gods they worship. And the heathen nations, though believing their deities to have power far surpassing man's, yet thought of them as using their power in such a way as any ordinarily good man would be ashamed to do ; beings jealous, selfish, capricious, impure, whom men might well fear, but few admire, and none could love. What must have been the purifying influence in the world of a religion which taught of one Father of all, rich in goodness and truth, in mercy and loving-kindness ? No wonder that proselytes from other nations should come to them unsought, convinced that their God alone deserved to be worshipped.

Yet when our Saviour came, how much of its savour the salt had lost ! The great truths were still acknowledged, but the life had so gone out of them in their practical application, that our Lord found His bitterest opponents in those who had the most bigoted attachment to their national law. They had lost all sense of proportion. They attached absurd importance to the observance of precepts concerning comparatively trivial matters, while the weighty matters were so neglected that the apostle could say of those who made their boast of the law, that they dishonoured God by their breaking of the law, and that instead of heathen peoples being attracted and influenced by their high example, the name of their God was evil spoken of by the Gentiles on their account. Thus, while they kept the body of their law, the life had gone out of it. The salt had lost its savour.

Through the preaching of our Lord and His apostles, there came a great reformation. In the Jewish nation it was perhaps only a minority that was influenced by it, but the barrier of exclusiveness that had separated that nation from others was broken down, and their light was permitted to shine abroad. Darkness had covered the earth, but the prophecies were fulfilled that the Gentiles should come to the Jewish light; that they who walked in darkness should see a great light, and that on those that dwelt in the land of the shadow of death the true light should shine. The result was that the new society became a chosen people, a holy nation; trustworthy and honest, when elsewhere it was hard to find one on whom dependence could be placed; pure in the midst of impurity; truthful when others scrupled not to lie. Such was the Christian Church at first, shining like a light in a dark place. Yet if we go down a century we find it fallen much from its high ideal. Even in the lifetime of the apostles the excellence of some was painfully contrasted with the shortcoming of many who were Christians, at least in name. We may, perhaps, not be surprised to hear that Paul, at quite an early period of his history, thinking of visiting Corinth, feared lest he should find among his disciples there, envyings, strifes, backbitings, whisperings, swellings, tumults, but we should hardly have expected that he should go on to say that he feared to have to bewail many who had sinned already,

and had not repented of the uncleanness and forni-
cation and lasciviousness which they had committed.
I need not quote from later Epistles, but a hundred
years after our Lord's death Christians were mourning over the defilements by which the once pure
Church had been stained, and were looking for
a new Gospel of repentance.

Yet, notwithstanding its shortcomings, the Church
had more to attract than to repel ; it triumphed over
persecution, and a Christian emperor sat on the
throne. We have records which enable us to draw
a picture of life in the capital which he founded, and
it much resembles what we should see in a luxurious
and dissipated city of our own time—a predominant
outward profession of Christianity, but scant observance of its precepts. We should not dream of calling
the Christianity which we saw there the salt which
was to purify the earth ; we should rather ask where
shall we find the salt to purify *it*. That which had
been salt in the apostles' times had now lost its
savour.

Attempts at such purification were made. Out of
the nominally Christian world, bands of men who
aimed at living a higher life collected themselves
into little societies which bid fair to be the salt to
purify the general immorality, and for a time really
were so. It is what we know of their virtues which
forbids our passing too sweeping a condemnation on
the age in which they lived. Their virtues shine all
the brighter by contrast with the dark background
of a society which had been deteriorated by the
withdrawal from its ordinary work of some of the
best and most God-regarding of its members. Yet

even in those little societies themselves the salt soon lost its savour. First there came, as in the Corinthian Church, strifes, debates, whisperings, backbitings, tumults. Their peace was disturbed by mutual jealousies; their zeal for truth passed into bitter intolerance; outsiders complained that in their zeal for the interests of their society they disregarded honesty and justice; worst of all, many of them became corrupted by the wealth which had been willingly poured on them in the days of their first devotion; self-denial passed into comfort, comfort into luxury, and that again into actual vice.

It would be too long to describe fully the successive attempts made to replace with fresh salt, salt that had lost its savour; but one great attempt deserves special mention, that which we commonly know as the Reformation. It was made at a time when all were agreed that the Church needed reform in its head and its members. And it was felt by many that the cause of the general corruption was the ignorance of the Word of God in which the people had been kept by their spiritual guides, and consequent reliance by those who had fallen into sin on false methods of restoration to the favour of God, which did not include forsaking of the sins which had to be acknowledged. And undoubtedly a deeper sense was inspired of the requirements of God's law, such that many showed the effects of this teaching in their lives, and did deserve to be called the salt of the earth; but, alas! there, too, there were many with whom the salt lost its savour. In fact, it is too common with men to accept intellectual enlightenment as a substitute for moral renovation, and, priding themselves in their more accurate knowledge of the truth, to neglect to show forth its influence in their lives. More especially is this the case if the truth is one for which it has been necessary to combat; for then the instinct of battle makes the contested object more dear, and there will be eagerness to retain it after it has lost its value. It has happened in some military engagements that it has been thought necessary to concentrate a defending force in order to maintain a threatened position, and that it has presently been overlooked that this was no longer the point of danger, and that consequently all has been lost by an attack on another quarter, against which no sufficient provision had been made. And still oftener has the like of this happened in theological as well as in political controversies. Men flatter themselves that they are fighting God's battles if they shout vigorously an old battle cry, and stand conspicuously on a part of the wall where no attack is being made. The worst of an imagination that we are doing God's work when it is not true that we are, is that men are apt to think that if they fulfil somewhat more perfectly than others their duty to God, it will atone for much shortcomings in their fulfilment of their duty to their neighbour.

It is an instructive fact that when our Lord was on earth, His severest rebukes were addressed to the most religious people of His day—the Pharisees who won the respect of all by their zeal for the law of God. And He regarded their religion as aggravating the sin of their wrong dealings. Men "who devour widows' houses, and for a pretence make long prayers, these shall receive the greater damnation." "For a pretence"—it may very possibly have been a pretence which imposed on themselves. Our Lord repeatedly accused them of being hypocrites—that is to say, according to the primary meaning of the word, "actors," and the most successful actors are those who can so throw themselves into their part as to banish from their own mind the thought that they are not really what they profess to be.

Our Lord said of those who hoped to make the goodness of their theory excuse the laxity of their practice, they shall receive the greater condemnation ; and is not that the verdict which our own public opinion passes ? There is nothing that men resent more than hypocrisy. Men whose own lives would incline them to pass a lenient judgment on vice, are not only shocked but angry when these vices are committed by those who have given reason to expect from them exceptional goodness. It seems to us a personal injury when an attempt has been made to swindle us out of undeserved respect and admiration. And we cannot doubt that in the sight of God, too, the hypocrite is judged to deserve greater condemnation when we see the injury done to the cause of religion by the misconduct of unworthy professors. The apostle Paul told those who boasted in the name of Jew, and yet transgressed the law in which they gloried, that through their means the name of God was blasphemed among the Gentiles. The same thing happens to every one whose life does not correspond to the name in which he glories, whether the name be Christian or Catholic or Protestant, or pious and religious. Just as there were Pharisees who made long prayers and devoured widows' houses, so there have been many pious plunderers since, who, indeed, owed their opportunities for plundering to the confidence reposed in their professions of piety. I remember well how some years ago, on the winding up of a swindling company, it was sworn that the directors had always opened their meetings with prayer; and the judge sarcastically asked, did they begin by saying, " Let us prey?" When men of high repute for piety are found out to be not better but worse than those who make no profession, even though the delinquents be comparatively few, the very name of religion comes to stink in men's nostrils; and those who themselves care little for religion, are apt to think that the profession of it is nothing but a cloak for deceit. I remember hearing of a very pious Roman Catholic whose parting counsel to his son was : " Never trust a man who goes to mass on a week-day." Thus the saying is true that the best thing, when it becomes corrupt, is the worst of all. The salt that has lost its savour is fit for nothing but to be cast out and trodden under foot. Men rid themselves of it as of a mouldering carcass from which life has fled. It is a fine thing for an institution, for a party, for a family, for a nation, to be able to boast of a glorious past, as long as it is animated by the spirit which originally won its fame. But if it is only in external features that the ancestral likeness has been preserved, the reminder of the past brings shame, not honour.

History tells of many vicissitudes in the rise and fall of nations. Our own century has exhibited some striking ones. The beginning witnessed the collapse of the nation whose military reputation had stood at the highest. The middle saw the recovery of the same power. Its close has beheld the dissolution of the Spanish empire of which it was first said that on it the sun never set. The history of decline and fall is that a nation which has done great deeds can live for a long time on the credit of its acquired reputation, and after its virtues have passed into routine, its energy departed, and its strength decayed, the character which it had won prevents men from seeing how little formidable it has now become. At length some vigorous young rival has courage to put the matter to the test; weakness is exposed, and sovereignty passes into other hands. The moral for ourselves is that we must not rely too much on the credit of past services, whether rendered by ourselves or by the party to which we may join ourselves. The question which practical men will ask is, What service are we capable of rendering *now* ? It may be that we labour on in an old groove, and are blind to a change of time, in consequence of which the services which in former times were useful are not what the present age requires. It may be a worse evil that we no longer maintain the spirit which inspired our ancestors, or which breathed in our own youth. Strive to keep fresh the life that is in you. Nothing more terrible can be said to any than : "Thou hast a name that thou livest and art dead."

SERMON XIV

TAKE HEED HOW YE HEAR

"Take heed how ye hear : for whosoever hath, to him shall be given ; and whosoever hath not, from him shall be taken away even that which he thinketh he hath."—LUKE viii. 18.

ON two different occasions our Lord warned His disciples of this rule of God's government of the world. There is something startling in it when it is thus enunciated, and we are tempted to cry out against it as unjust. What, give to those who least want a gift! take from those who are worst able to spare to part with anything! Can anything be more unlike all we know of our Lord's character than that He should approve the principle of stripping the poor in order to add unneeded luxury to the rich?

Yet it is difficult to deny that this actually is the rule by which the world is governed. "Much will have more" is one of those sayings in which men pack into a short proverb the result of multiplied experience. Sometimes it happens in real life as well as in legendary tales, that a man comes to London with the proverbial half-crown in his pocket, and finishes with wealth enough to satisfy the dreams of avarice : when such a one tells the history of his progress, you find that the first years were a time of previously acquainted. That information, which by an ignorant person would have been received at best with indolent curiosity, and have been forgotten as soon as learned, becomes to him a key which opens the door to many new chambers of knowledge; or, to employ our Lord's own illustration, that talent for which the ignorant person could find no better use than to hide it away, wrapped up in a napkin, if entrusted to a wealthy banker, is made to yield profitable interest.

I said that we read of our Lord on two occasions enunciating the general principle of what I have been speaking. The first was in connection with the parable of the sower, the second in connection with another parable which He probably spoke on different occasions, for it seems to have reached the evangelists, Matthew and Luke, through different channels. They give different versions of it, the lessons conveyed being in the two substantially the same, but the details being somewhat different. Matthew's parable we know as the parable of the Talents, Luke's as that of the Pounds. Does it seem unjust to you in the parable that the one talent should be taken away from him who had gained nothing by it? Is it not what we see in daily life—that faculties unused decay, and in time are lost; that opportunities neglected, do not present themselves again? Does it seem strange that it should be exactly the man who had only one talent who had not employed it? But who is it that is assailed by the temptation, "not worth while," but those who can do but little? Why, this is a form that the benevolence of our age has taken, by the institution of Penny Savings Banks, and by the acceptance at the Post-Office from children of their collection of postage stamps, to educate people into the conviction that it is worth while to make even a saving that seems absolutely insignificant, and so be trained into a habit that is sure to grow.

Does it seem strange that to him who had already had most, a new talent should be entrusted? Yet who is most likely to open up a new way of doing good to the souls or bodies of men? Is it not one who has most largely used the well-known means of usefulness? Charitable collectors know this well, and when they want to beg for a new object, they go in preference to those who have most largely contributed to the old ones.

What underlies our Lord's whole method of teaching by parables is that the laws of God's government are uniform : the method which we find to prevail in one department may fitly be used to illustrate another. This uniformity of Nature is the keynote of all modern science. If there was not this analogy between the laws of the kingdom which Christ founded and the laws of the natural world, might we not have cause to doubt whether the God of Christianity were the same as the God of Nature?

Thus, then, the laws which regulate the acquirement of knowledge are the same, whether the knowledge be purely intellectual, or religious, or spiritual. The chapter from which I took my text, and which we read as the lesson for to-day, records the circumstances under which the words of the text were then spoken. Our Lord had been asked why He reserved His full instructions for His disciples, and only spoke to the cultivator has had at first better reason for hope. Often does it happen, for example, that a teacher finds in his class a young man who gives such token both of ability and of liking for his subject, that he has good reason to anticipate that his studies will be successful. There is in this case no lack of interest, and, at first, no unwillingness to spend labour in the pursuit; but the learner falls into society where he is introduced to amusements which have more attraction for him than the study on which he had embarked; his zeal relaxes, and his teacher's hopes are blighted. Such a case is in the intellectual world the exact counterpart of that which in the sphere of religion is described in the parable as represented by the seed cast into thorny ground. Though the good seed had been received with joy, and sprung up, and at first gave good promise of fruit, yet as time went on the pleasures and cares and ambitions of this world gained an ascendancy of attractive power, and so the word was choked, and became unfruitful.

I took my text from St Luke's version of the parable of the sower rather than from the corresponding passage in St Matthew, because St Luke records words omitted by St Matthew, and yet which are necessary in order to exhibit the practical object with which the parable of the sower was spoken, in the words, "Take heed how ye hear." For want of attention to these words, many who have commented on the parable have treated it as if it were only meant to throw light on the speculative difficulty, how it is that the divinely uttered lessons of our Lord could fail to produce saving effect. And no doubt it does throw light on that difficulty. It teaches that if fruit does not spring, it is from no fault or weakness in the seed. That which yields a hundredfold is the same as that which is trampled down on the wayside or devoured by the fowls of the air. The difference results altogether from the difference of the soil in which it is cast.

When the parable was looked at exclusively from a theoretical point of view, the question has been asked, how far it harmonises with modern systems of theology. For instance, what is meant by an honest and good heart? Considering what we are told in Scripture about the wickedness of man's heart, can any human heart be described as honest and good? But there is no difficulty in understanding our Lord's meaning, if we remember that He was not composing a scientific treatise on theology, but speaking in popular language with a practical object. Is there anything better known than that the effect of anything that is said depends chiefly on the disposition of mind of him who hears, whether, for instance, what is told him agrees with what he had previously believed or suspected to be true; whether, again, the speaker is one whom he admires and trusts, and to whose statements and arguments therefore he will give a favourable hearing, even though they oblige him to alter previously conceived opinions; or whether, again, those previous opinions can be shown to conflict with feelings in the hearers' breasts to which the speaker knows how to appeal? Thus eloquence lies far less in the lips of the orator than in the ears of the listener. How many an eloquent oration has been listened to with admiration, but has inspired no action. The prophet of old had an ex-

perience which has been repeated to many a speaker
and preacher since, when he complained of hearers to
whom he was but the very lovely song of one who
hath a pleasant voice and can play well on an
instrument; for they hear his words and do them
not.

On the other hand, it has often happened that one
who has no great gifts of eloquence has said some un-
pretending words which have come home to his hearers'
hearts, and, stored up there, have been an abiding
influence for good.   When a violinist draws his bow
over his instrument in proximity to the strings of a
piano, the string will vibrate which is in harmony
with the note sounded, while all the others are dumb.
Thus what our Lord says about the need of an
honest and good heart teaches no different lesson
from that contained in the saying of the wise man,
which I already quoted, about the fool in whose hands
is put a price to get wisdom, but who has no heart
for it.

Thus our Lord in His discourse justifies His
conduct in making known the mysteries of His
kingdom, not to the mixed crowd of careless
bystanders, but to select disciples who had shown
themselves attentive and eager listeners.   But to them,
too, the warning must be given: Do *you* take heed
how *you* hear.   Their hearts had not been hardened
by roadside indifference; but they might be full of
noxious weeds which in their growth would smother
up the fruit of the good seed.   And this we know in
at least one case actually happened.   Whether the
crime of Judas was inspired by avarice, as the Gospel
history would suggest, or, as some modern speculators

have imagined, from disappointed ambition, or from a desire that the exigencies of peril should force our Lord into an exercise of supernatural power, which would put Him into His proper place as a temporal ruler; in any case, there clearly were in the heart of the traitor apostle noxious weeds which found there a more congenial soil than that which had been shown by our Lord.

The practical lesson then remains for you, "Take heed how ye hear." If you would be worthy hearers of the Word, you must prepare your hearts so that they may be fitted for its reception; you must break up the hard and stony ground; you must weed out the choking thorns. True the preparations of the heart are from God. But God acts through the wills of men, not in violation of their freedom; and He has left it possible for them to commit the sin with which Jews of old were charged by the preacher, who cried: "Ye do always resist the Holy Ghost; as your fathers did, so do ye."

On the other hand, when St James gave the exhortation: "Cleanse your hands, ye sinners, and purify your hearts, ye double-minded," he taught at the same time how that was to be done, by joining the exhortations, "Resist the Devil, and he will flee from you: draw near to God, and He will draw near to you." Which is it you will resist—the godly motions of the Holy Spirit striving with you, or the temptations with which the Evil One would seduce you? for if you will, it is in your power to resist either successfully.

God grant you grace to choose the better part: grace to repel Satan, so that the baffled tempter will retire, grace to draw near to Him who is ever more ready to give than you to ask, who freely bestows His Holy Spirit on those who seek it, who will give you singleness of heart, casting out every root of bitterness, and thus so preparing the soil that the good seed will bear fruit a hundredfold.

SERMON XV

TRIALS AND TEMPTATIONS

"Wherein ye greatly rejoice, though now for a season, if need be, ye are in heaviness through manifold temptations, that the trial of your faith, being much more precious than of gold that perisheth, though it be tried with fire, might be found unto praise and honour and glory at the appearing of Jesus Christ."

—I PETER i. 6, 7.

THE text contains two words, trials and temptations, which, as far as their etymology is concerned, ought to mean nearly the same thing, but as generally used, convey very different ideas, and indeed are used without much thought about their etymology. When people talk of having had trials, they mean that they have had to suffer affliction or distress, and the use of the phrase generally indicates that they think of them as sent by the hand of God for some mysterious reason that they do not presume to fathom. Temptations, on the other hand, are looked on as altogether evil things coming from the Devil, or at least from the world or the flesh, and not from God; and they seem to have for thinking so, the authority of St James, who says: "Let no man say when he is tempted, I am tempted of God: for God cannot be tempted of evil, neither tempteth He any man: but every man is tempted, when he is drawn away of his own lust, and enticed."

173

Yet etymologically, the word "temptation" means no more than "trial"; and the Greek word which is commonly translated "tempt" or "temptation," very often cannot be so rendered without conveying quite a wrong idea to an English reader. Thus when our Lord, in reference to the hungry multitudes, said to Philip, "Whence shall we buy bread that these may eat?" our translators render St John's comment: "This He said to *prove* him, for He Himself knew what He would do," for it would evidently convey a false idea if they had rendered, "This He said to tempt him." In the text when St Peter says to his disciples that they were in heaviness through manifold temptations, perhaps "trials" would have more nearly conveyed the idea to us, for what St Peter had in view was the persecution which they had to endure. No doubt, persecution did bring with it a certain temptation, namely, that of escaping it by apostasy. But the apostle's meaning comes out none more clearly in a following passage (iv. 12), where the same word, commonly translated tempt, occurs, "Beloved, think it not strange concerning the fiery trial which is to try you, as though some strange thing happened to you." Here the Revised Version renders "which is to *prove* you." There is in fact a word common enough in books of theology, though not quite so common in ordinary language, which expresses the idea, namely, that we are here in a state of *probation*, our characters being continually tried and proved; it may be by what we ordinarily call temptations, when inducements are held out to us to do wrong, and our conduct reveals whether or no we have firmness to resist them; it may be by what we ordinarily call trials, when what is proved is not so much whether we have firmness to resist as whether we have strength to bear. Nay, it may be by wealth and prosperity which no less than adversity bring a trial. So felt one of old, who prayed that he might not be exposed to trial of either kind. He asked: "Give me neither poverty nor riches, lest I be full and deny Thee, and say, who is the Lord, or lest I be poor, and steal, and take the name of the Lord in vain."

Now here is one of the paradoxes of Scripture. If I had wished to put it before you in a striking way, I might have prefixed two texts to my sermon; on the one hand, the petition of our Lord's prayer, "Lead us not into temptation"; on the other hand, the saying of St James, i. 3. "My brethren, count it all joy when ye fall into divers temptations." Yet surely there is good reason for both views. With regard to what we ordinarily call trials, none of us can wish to fall under the chastening hand of God. Even though we know that, as the apostle says, chastening afterwards yields the peaceable fruit of righteousness unto them that have been exercised thereby, the same apostle owns that no chastening for the present seems joyous, but grievous. Still more with regard to what we ordinarily call temptations, conscious as we are of our weakness, we may reasonably dread a conflict in which there is danger of our being worsted. Yet one who has been subjected to either kind of trial, and in the Lord's strength has sustained it firmly and successfully, has cause to rejoice at the discipline he has undergone. Nor have we reason to think that our Father has dealt ill with us in subjecting us to it. To think so would be to find fault with the whole constitution of the world. It is by exercise and trial that all our faculties are proved and strengthened. Who could expect good work from muscles that had grown flabby from disuse? What general would like to encounter an army of veterans, if he himself commanded only feather-bed soldiers, who had been lapped in luxury, and until then had never seen the face of an enemy? The whole constitution of the world is that we are not made at first what we are intended to be; we grow into it, and our growth is shaped and directed by the circumstances in which we are placed and the influences that surround us. Before we can do our work in the world, we have to pass through the long preliminary training of childhood, during which our strength and our faculties are developed, we are taught the lessons most needful for us to know, and are subjected to the discipline which will enable us to conquer indolence and self-will. So that it is quite of a piece with the whole constitution of the world, that we are not created fit to enter on the life of eternity without the training given in our childhood season of preparation in this life, during which, if we use it rightly, we grow into likeness with Him, to dwell with whom, and to be like whom, will constitute our happiness hereafter.

Now, if our discipline here included nothing but what we popularly call trials, I do not think we should feel that we had any reason to doubt the goodness of God, or to hesitate to believe the saying that He does not afflict willingly. We can all recognise that valuable lessons may be learned in the school of adversity. There is felt to be something incomplete in the character of one with whom everything has gone smoothly, and who has never known sorrow or anxiety. That jovial high-spirited man may be a pleasant companion in our lighter hours, but is it to him we would turn for advice in our own anxiety, or for sympathy in our own affliction? Any one who has passed through the discipline of affliction must know that he has been there taught lessons which it was good for him to have learned. Now, surely no child would have a right to think his father was not good to him because he sets him some lessons to learn which he finds repulsive or difficult, or which he cannot, at the time, see the use of.

But trials such as we ordinarily call temptations seem to stand on a different footing, for these involve real danger, to which it seems hard that we should be exposed. Yet when the danger has been faced and encountered successfully, we can feel ourselves the better of the trial. We have been tested in small matters and have been found faithful; we have thus proved our right to be entrusted with greater charges, and may with courage undertake them in good hope that when the test comes we shall not be found wanting. What soldier thinks his commander does him an injury in choosing him for a post of danger? Nay, he feels honoured by his commander's confidence that his courage and his presence of mind will not fail, and he accepts the trust, resolved that they shall not. And such were the feelings of those who passed through the severest temptation of all, the temptation to deny Christ when called on to confess Him before the hostile tribunal. The valiant confessors of old murmured not that it should be their lot to encounter such a trial, but gloried in the honour done them, as

M

we are told of the apostles who, when beaten for their confession of Christ, rejoiced that they had been counted worthy to suffer shame for His name. God, we are told, is like a refiner's fire, and those who have passed through it may echo the Psalmist's thanksgiving: " Thou hast tried us as silver is tried. We went through fire and through water, but Thou broughtest us out into a wealthy place."

But what of those who fail?

Well, if we could give no account at all of this matter, we might well hesitate, even if we had the power, to change the existing constitution of things according to which men's energies are braced by conflict. It cannot be called a conflict if a combatant is, like the hero of some legends, cased in impenetrable armour, or is made invulnerable; still less, if he is wrapped up in wadding and forbidden to enter the fight at all. Now, if to do away with conflict does away with the possibility of defeat, it does away also with the possibility of victory, and it may well be doubted whether to gain the certainty that none should fail would not be too dearly purchased by the certainty that none could succeed.

But it is important to bear in mind that trial does not bring weakness; it only brings it to light. If when the metal is placed in the furnace a quantity of dross is found in it, it is not the fire that causes the dross, it only reveals what had been there before. Now, if the object of the discipline of this life is to remove our defects, and make us more fit to do God's work, it is clearly not desirable that our defects should remain undetected. It is far better that they should be revealed to ourselves, even though they are at the same time revealed to others, too. In the absence of trial or temptation, we know little of the characters of ourselves or others. How could we possibly compare the characters of two different men if we only know what they have done, and do not know also the temptations to which each has been subjected. He whose character seems to us the most spotless, might perchance have failed more signally than the other, had he been subjected to a like temptation. But if there be any flaw in a man's character, it is hard for him to live long in the world without having it exposed, as a strain is put on it by the different vicissitudes of life. But the really important thing is that the revelation should be made to himself. How little do we know of our own characters! While life flows on with us in a prosperous current, and temptations are weak, and we are called on to resign or avoid nothing that we much care to forego, on what good terms we can be with our consciences, how thankful we can imagine ourselves to be to God for His mercies, how willing to show forth His praise in the way which He has appointed; and then when we least expect it, temptation comes, and we are startled and ashamed by finding that it overcomes us. It may be the allurements of forbidden pleasure unexpectedly presented which overpower our caution; it may be some trifling offence which stirs up our anger, and we speak unadvisedly with our lips, and are hurried into unchristian bitterness; it may be some pecuniary interest at stake which causes us to swerve from our direct course; it may be that when we are

keep, in the books you read, in the indulgences you
allow yourself, harmless, possibly, in the case of others,
but if safe for them not safe for you.   If by precau-
tions of this kind you weaken your enemy so as to get
the victory over him, every such victory brings an
increase of strength whereby you may be able to
encounter successfully temptations that had triumphed
over you before.   And believe it, God does not send
temptations that they should conquer you, but that
you should conquer them, and if you encounter them
in His strength, you will find His promise true—that
He will not suffer you to be tried above that you are
able, but will, with the temptation, make a way to
escape that you may be able to bear it.

SERMON XVI

THE HISTORIC CLAIMS OF EPISCOPACY [1]

"The things that thou hast heard of me among many witnesses, the same commit thou to faithful men, who shall be able to teach others also."—2 TIMOTHY ii. 2.

IT has been customary with defenders of the Christian faith to challenge those who deny the fact of our Lord's Resurrection to say what they think of the men who first preached that doctrine. Were they deceivers or deceived? Could they have been innocently mistaken, or did they propagate a story which they knew not to be true? I do not know that any unbeliever now denies the perfect sincerity of the Apostolic preachers. Their writings that remain to us bear a stamp of strong conviction, which it is impossible to dispute. In this point of view, a special value attaches to the Pastoral Epistles of St Paul. These are not letters addressed to the outside public; they are the confidential communications that passed between the most successful preacher of the new religion and his chief assistants. Stories have been told of infidel priests of our religion in later times, who, when they were by themselves, made no secret

[1] Preached in St Mary's Cathedral, Edinburgh, on St Matthew's Day, 1886, at the consecration of John Dowden, D.D., Bishop of Edinburgh.

of their unbelief, but boasted how gainful the fable had been to them. But we cannot seriously discuss the suggestion that worldly advantage could have prompted the exertions of Paul and his fellow-labourers. The Christian missionary then had to look forward to loss of property, loss of liberty, loss of character. The letter from which the text is taken was written from prison, and Paul intimates that the sting of the imprisonment was that he suffered as an evil-doer : in other words, that in the eyes of all who did not know him well, he was regarded as a common malefactor, suffering the just punishment of his crimes. And he had no better prospect to offer his disciple. He tells him, that " all that will live godly in Christ Jesus shall suffer persecution." He invites him to be " partaker of the afflictions of the Gospel "; he exhorts him to " endure hardness as a good soldier of Christ," and not to be ashamed of the suffering which the testimony would bring. Paul's support under his trials arose from the strength of his faith in the cause for which he cared more than for himself. He was bound, but he rejoices that " the word of God was not bound." " I am not ashamed," he says, " for I know whom I have believed, and am persuaded that He is able to keep that which I have committed unto Him against that day."

You will easily understand, however, that, in taking my text from this Epistle now, it was not my object to produce evidence of the strong faith which the apostle Paul had in the Gospel which he preached. On an occasion like the present, it is to these Epistles the preacher naturally turns, whether his object is to treat of the theory of the Christian ministry, or to speak practically of the dignity of the office, and of the responsibility and duties which it imposes. With respect to the theory of the Christian ministry, the Pastoral Epistles are particularly valuable, because they are the latest of Paul's Epistles. In studying the history of the first years of the Church, we might, perhaps, be at a loss to judge how much was to be regarded as exceptional, as special to the time when the Church was governed by apostles endowed with miraculous powers; but these Epistles bring us down to the time when the apostle was, as he says, " now ready to be offered," and when the care of the Churches he had founded was to be handed over to the men of the second generation ; and they give evidence that several of what have been imagined to be later developments existed in Apostolic times. The aspect which these Epistles present of a fully organised Church, with gradations of officers, is enough to dispel the dreams of those who would have us believe that the whole institution of the Christian ministry is an unscriptural invasion of the rights of the laity, every one of whom, we do not deny, is bound to be a preacher of righteousness, and is entitled to regard himself as a priest unto God, fully authorised, without the intervention of any human mediator, to present his supplications before the mercy-seat of God. There are those who regard the mutual relations between Christians as only resembling that between the particles of a mass of gravel or sand, all of like nature, but otherwise independent of each other ; or, if a comparison to inanimate objects be deemed inappropriate, like that between flowers in a bed, in proximity with each other, but each enjoying its own independent life ; or (if even this illustration be regarded as inadequate) like that between fellow-travellers who chance to be going the same road, all, no doubt, having the same goal in view, all willing to bestow kind and courteous help on the others, but in other respects completely independent of the rest, and without any pretensions to be regarded as a corporate body. I think this last illustration adequately represents a very popular view of the Christian Church, and you will see how very much it falls below the Apostolic illustration, which represents Christians as members of an organised body, all drawing their nourishment from a common source, but each member having its proper functions, and each in fullest sympathy with the others. When we once understand that the Scriptural conception of the Church is not that of an aggregate of particles identical in nature, like grains of sand, or flowers in a bed, but of an organised body, the parts of which have differentiated functions, there is no difficulty in receiving the doctrine that the Church is a corporate body, having its rulers and officers, and that there are some of its members to whom the special function is assigned of teaching and directing others.

In conformity with this is the whole Scripture history of the early Church. We are told of our Lord's appointing twelve to be His first missionaries. But their work was not limited to what He sent them to perform in His lifetime. We find from the Acts, that after His death, they remained the rulers and governors of the society which He had formed. We find that they filled up a vacancy in their number. We are told that, in every Church which they founded,

they appointed elders. These elders did not obtain
their office by the natural right of being the oldest
or the leading men of the community, but by a
solemn ordination. St Luke's words are: "They
ordained them elders in every city, and having
prayed, with fasting, they commended them to the
Lord, on whom they believed" (Acts xiv. 23). And
now, in these Epistles, which give us almost our farewell view of the Apostolic Churches, we find that
Timothy, who had been admitted to his office by a
like solemn ordination, is commissioned to ordain in
like manner a new series of elders.

There are three words in the text, the full force
of which a hasty reader might overlook. Timothy,
we know, was a convert and a disciple of Paul's.
Paul calls him his "own son in the faith." He had,
no doubt, fully instructed him in the doctrines of
the faith. If there were no such thing as an
organized Church, and if Paul were but the head
of a school, like Plato or Aristotle, it would still be
natural for him to wish, that one whom he had fully
taught his doctrines should communicate them to a
new generation. This was the view of apostolic
traditions taken by some early heretics. They
thought that the apostles communicated their
doctrines privately to their disciples, and these
again to others; and the Gnostic teachers professed
to be in possession of these secret Apostolic traditions. But the Scriptures justify no such view.
Whatever instruction Paul had privately given to
Timothy—and, no doubt, he must have given much
—he makes no reference to it here. What he reminds him of is the things he had heard "before

many witnesses." There are extremely many
phrases common to the two Epistles to Timothy
and that to Titus, such as to afford clear evidence
that the three letters were written by the same
person, and at no great distance of time from one
another. One of these phrases is this, " before many
witnesses." We find it again in the first Epistle to
Timothy (vi. 12), but there is a slightly different
connection, so as to show that the one phrase is
not a mere copy of the other. The first Epistle
speaks of the good profession which Timothy had
professed before many witnesses.[1] It is clear from
the two passages that Paul is not reminding Timothy
of any private instruction he had given him, but of
a solemn ordination, in which Paul had, in the
face of the Church, given him in charge the
doctrines which he was to teach; and Timothy
had equally, in the face of the Church, professed
his belief in these doctrines. We find also, from two
other passages (1 Tim. iv. 14; 2 Tim. i. 6), that hands
were then solemnly laid on Timothy by Paul himself, and, as it would appear, by the presbyters of
the Church also, and that, through that laying on
of hands, a gift was communicated, not one to be
enjoyed indolently, but which needed to be diligently
exercised. " Neglect not the gift that is in thee,
which was given thee by prophecy, with the laying
on of the hands of the presbytery." " Stir up the gift
of God, which is in thee by the putting on of my
hands."

---

[1] The definite article ("thou didst confess *the* good confession") indicates that that to which Timothy professed his
adherence was a statement of doctrine, well known and
honoured among Christians.

There are those who will readily acknowledge that an apostle was entitled to exercise authority over Churches, and especially over Churches which he had founded himself, and who would account for the authority exercised by Timothy by the supposition that Paul, during a temporary absence, delegated some of his authority to his disciple. But the whole of the Epistle leads us to regard Timothy, not as a private delegate of Paul, but as an officer of the Church, holding a post to which he had been publicly admitted by solemn rite, with the assent of the whole congregation.

But what was the office to which Timothy was thus solemnly appointed? Was it merely that of elder or presbyter? Two things show that it was something more. First, it appears to have been part of Timothy's office to receive and judge of accusations against presbyters. St Paul directs him to be cautious against regarding ill-attested rumours against an elder's character; but if the charge be proved by the testimony of two or three witnesses, he is publicly to rebuke them that sin before all, in order that others also may fear (1 Tim. v. 19, 20). The second point is the responsibility that appears to be thrown on Timothy singly with regard to the ordination of new presbyters. The text speaks of the solemn charge in which he was to hand on to them the deposit of doctrine that had been committed to himself. An earlier chapter describes the qualifications which he is to require in those who were to be admitted to the ministerial office. Timothy is warned against committing the sacred charge to a novice untried in the faith. He is warned also against precipitancy in his choice. He must lay hands suddenly on no man (1 Tim. iii. 6 ; v. 22). In connection with these passages, we must consider what Paul says in the Epistle to Titus (i. 5) : "For this cause left I thee in Crete, that thou shouldest set in order the things that are wanting, and ordain elders in every city, as I had appointed thee."

If we had not Scripture evidence to the contrary, we might imagine that the presiding officers of the Church were developed by spontaneous generation in each Christian community. The little society would, of course, need officers to conduct its affairs, and we might suppose that the Church would look out the most trusted of its members, who would probably be, as the name implies, the elder, and that it would set these persons to rule over them. But the New Testament informs us that, however probable it may be that the voice of the Church was heard in selecting candidates for ordination, the ultimate appointment was made by a higher authority. In the Acts, it is the Apostolic missionaries who are related to have ordained elders in each Church; and in these Pastoral Epistles the ordination is described as made by men possessing authority derived from an apostle, but not apostles themselves. The office of rule over presbyters, held by Timothy, corresponds to that to which, in somewhat later times, the name bishop was appropriated ; for in the earliest age of the Church that name had not this special signification, but appears to have been used as synonymous with elder or presbyter. But since we are concerned not with the name but the thing, there is full justification for what our Church asserts in the Preface to the Ordinal, that " it is evident unto all men diligently reading the Scriptures and ancient authors, that from the apostles' times there have been these orders of ministers in Christ's Church—bishops, priests, and deacons."

Some part of the Scripture evidence has been already touched on. This place would not be suitable for a discussion of what is said by ancient authors, but a few words on the subject may properly be said. Immediately after the Apostolic times Church history, as it were, passes through a tunnel. There is bright light on the history as long as we have the New Testament to guide us, and there is bright light again when we come down to the copious Christian literature, which began to be plentiful towards the end of the second century. But there is a comparatively dark intervening period, of which we have but few records ; for the generation that immediately succeeded the apostles does not seem to have included many men of literary ability, and the Church was then pressed by persecution, and eagerly looking forward to the second coming of their Lord. So it has happened that the greater part of the scanty literary remains of the sub-apostolic age is taken up with the controversy with heathenism and Judaism, and tells us little about the internal constitution of the Church. It is a great convenience to ingenious speculators to be unchecked by documentary evidence, and accordingly the attempt has been made to form a theory of Church government by disregarding the

periods concerning which the evidence is copious
and attending only to that dark period where the
scantiness of the evidence puts little restraint on
conjecture.[1] But it is a common experience with

[1] In writing this, I had in my mind Dr Hatch's Bampton
Lectures, the method of which is, in investigating the history
of early Church organisation, to set aside not only the later
evidence, but also that furnished by the New Testament
writers (see p. 20). If it were not for this exclusion of evidence, it would have been impossible to maintain the paradox propounded in the second lecture that the primary
signification of the name ἐπίσκοπος was the financial ad-
ministrator of the funds of the community. It is true that
as time went on, Christian liberality accumulated funds for
religious and charitable uses, the custody and distribution
of which formed a principal part of the bishop's cares. But
for the primary signification of the word in the Christian
society, we must look to the earliest instances of its use ; these
are to be found in the New Testament, and there it is apparent that the name has reference mainly to the spiritual
oversight of the flock over which the bishop has charge. In
the qualifications for the office enumerated in the Pastoral
Epistles, the power of teaching has a prominent part (see
in particular Titus i. 9). In one of the first places where the
word occurs, St Paul's address to the Ephesian elders, he
exhorts them "to take heed to the flock over which the
Holy Ghost had made them ἐπισκόπους," not to manage
their finances irreproachably, but "to feed the Church of
God, which He had purchased with His own blood." Similar
inferences may be drawn from a parallel passage (1 Peter
v. 2), and we need not doubt that it is the same officers who
are described in Heb. xiii. 17, as ἡγούμενοι, their duty being
to watch for the souls of their flock as men who must
give an account. And that shepherding was the primary
function of the ἐπίσκοπος is evident from St Peter's description
of our Lord (ii. 25) as "the Shepherd and Bishop of our
souls," a phrase which would have been ludicrous if it had
conveyed to the minds of the apostle's readers the idea of a
financial manager.

those who grope in dark chambers to come out covered with cobwebs, and I fear that no more complimentary epithet can be applied to speculations in which the best part of the evidence is systematically set aside. For those who desire to trace the history of Episcopacy during the feebly-illumined period of Church history, materials are not wanting, especially now that the genuineness of the Ignatian Epistles has been demonstrated to the satisfaction of all competent critics ; but I desire now to keep completely clear of the region where conjecture has been allowed to enter, and to confine myself to the facts about which there can be no dispute.

Now, when Christian literature becomes plentiful towards the end of the second century, we find the attention of the Church chiefly occupied with controversy with the Gnostic heretics, who, as I have already said, claimed to have derived, by secret tradition from the apostles, doctrines unknown to the universal Church. Two ways of meeting them were employed. One was to point out the unreasonableness of the supposition that the apostles, when they taught the Church publicly, either did not then know the whole truth, or wilfully kept back part of it from their disciples. But there was another way, namely, to prove that whatever the apostles taught, secret or public, the Church had better means of knowing it than their heretical opponents. And, accordingly, historical proof was offered that the Church then must be in full possession of Apostolic tradition, because the bishops who then ruled it could trace their descent by direct succession from the apostles. It was with this object that pains

N

were taken to trace the succession of bishops in the principal sees up to the very times when apostles founded them. I shall not trouble myself to discuss whether these ancient lists of bishops are completely trustworthy. It is sufficient for my purpose to say that when the Church comes out of the tunnel, of which I spoke, into the full light of history, we find bishops ruling everywhere, and no one having the least suspicion that since the apostles' times any other form of Church government had prevailed.

Two things lead me to think that they were not wrong in their belief. If the original form of government had been different, I cannot think that a change would have been universal, or that it could be silent. There would surely be found in some places survivals of the primitive form, and other places where the primitive form had not been changed without a struggle. If domineering or exceptionally gifted men in some places set themselves above their fellows, this would not happen everywhere, and surely the usurpation would in some places be so resisted that we could not help hearing of it. The presumption that the Church of the second century was not mistaken in its belief in the Apostolic origin of an Institution, which in that early age had obtained universal and uncontested acceptance, is confirmed when we turn to the New Testament.[1] I will not repeat what I have said

[1] We use the very same argument in establishing the New Testament canon itself. It is only at the end of the second century that the evidence becomes copious and beyond dispute. It is the full light that then prevails, reflected back on the

about Timothy and Titus. But there is one Church about which the New Testament tells us much—the Church of Jerusalem. And I do not think it can reasonably be disputed that the New Testament notices of that Church fully bear out the ancient tradition, that it was presided over by a single person, namely, St James. Thus I consider that the assertion of the Prayer-book is entirely justified, that that threefold ministry, which we still employ, dates back from Apostolic times.

The Prayer-book does not say that Episcopacy is so essential that without it the being of a Church is impossible; and I do not feel myself called on to go beyond what the Church has asserted. I own that there are some usages of the Apostolic Church which no Church at the present day observes; and in matters where Scripture contains no express command, I will not undertake to limit the power of the Church, to modify its institutions so as to adapt them better to the changing conditions of successive ages. When this concession has been made, I do not think that there is much in what I have stated which learned and candid Presbyterians would be unwilling to grant. There was a time when the parity of presbyters was maintained as the sole permissible form of Church government, and when prelacy was denounced as an un-Christian

earlier evidence, which enables us to set aside all cavils. We urge that it is incredible that a change in the Church's opinion could take place silently and universally; and we refuse to believe that the books universally held in honour at the period of which I speak, could have then newly come into existence, or could be different from those held in honour in the generation before.

usurpation. But I think such language is now only heard from unlearned persons who blindly repeat a traditional formula. Those Presbyterians who are entitled to be listened to with respect, rather take the line that Episcopacy is a form under which the constitution of the Church developed itself in confessedly very early times; yet not by Divine command, but only through the natural shaping of circumstances, and therefore free to be altered as circumstances alter.

But it may be doubted whether the older school of Presbyterians had not the truer sense of the exigencies of their position. They felt that no light grounds could justify the breaking up the unity of the Church. If forms of Church government were really left by Scripture matters of indifference, they would be no adequate causes of separation. I have spoken already of the idea prevalent at the present day, that the unity of the Church is no more than that of fellow-travellers on the same road, who sufficiently show their community of interest by an occasional kindly word, or a friendly act now and then. But this certainly is not the Scriptural conception of the Church. And the popular notion that outward divisions do the Church no harm, is thoroughly refuted by experience. A machine is known to be a bad one if, instead of its whole power going to do the work for which it was intended, the greater part of the power is spent in generating heat by friction between the component parts of the machine. Is not that a true picture of the actual history of the divided Church? How much of the energy that ought to have been spent on dispelling the ignorance and vice that is in the world has been expended by Christians in their mutual conflicts, one body of Christians being as pleased to make a convert from another body of Christians as if they had made the truth come home to the heart of a heathen or an infidel ; and heathens and infidels themselves assigning as their reason for refusing to listen to the claims of Christianity, that if they thought of accepting them they should be at a loss in choosing between different bodies of Christians, all of whom agreed in teaching that a wrong choice would be nearly as perilous to their souls as if they remained in heathenism. The exaggeration of the importance of points of difference springs from a secret consciousness of the sinfulness of schism. I could easily raise a smile if I were to give you a list of causes for which Christian unity has been broken, many of the points of difference being such that to our ideas it seems absurd to imagine that they could justify schism. But at least the parties to the disputes represented these matters as important, and declared themselves to be animated by concern for the safety of souls endangered by the use of faulty ceremonial. That such matters should be represented as vital testifies, as I have said, to the unconscious feeling of the contending parties that unless the points of difference were vital, schism would not be justified.

But, in fact to prove schism to be sinful, it is enough to show what injury it has done the Church. All God's laws are written deep in the constitution of nature. The moralist who sets himself to examine what things injure the human body and injure human society, will find that the things which he is thus led to condemn are exactly the things which God's law pronounces to be sins. So that when we convince ourselves of the enormous impediments to the progress of Christianity which the divisions of Christians have caused, we may be sure that the rending Christ's body is a sin, even if Scripture had not directly told us so. Supposing, then, proof completely to fail that Episcopacy is Apostolic, or that it is binding on the Church for all time, it no more follows that what was for so many ages the established constitution of the Church could at pleasure be overthrown, than it follows, that if we abandon the doctrine of the divine right of kings, we assert the right of rebellion against our present Sovereign.

I am far from imagining that a schism can be healed the moment that thoughtful men have come to regret that it has ever taken place, or at least to see that whatever grounds there might have been for it in the past, the points of difference are not such as now to justify disunion. It is far easier to make a schism than to heal it again. So the wise man said, " The beginning of strife is as when one letteth out water: therefore leave off contention, before it be meddled with." In the course of a long controversy things will be said and done on both sides which sound reason does not approve. Principles will be pushed to extremes ; strong assertions will be rashly made, tempting for the discomfiture of opponents, and always most acceptable to the less educated of their own party, who are apt to care far more that an assertion should be strong than that it should be strictly true. And human passions arise: those who differ from us are apt to be regarded as enemies, and to be treated as such when opportunity arises.

I have neither time nor inclination to trace the history of the long struggle between Episcopacy and Presbyterianism in Scotland, to balance the account of wrongs mutually inflicted, or to determine which party has now most to forgive. But when the fathers have eaten sour grapes, it cannot be but that the children's teeth should be set on edge. Resentments have been stirred up which cannot easily be allayed, nor can the uneducated easily be taught to unlearn their old shibboleths. When thoughtful men are anxious to retire from untenable positions, the uneducated imagine that a cowardly surrender of truth has been made. For these reasons I do not venture to hope that anything immediate can be done in the way of healing of schisms. But not the less do I think that we may take hopeful augury for the future from the increasing desire of thoughtful men for greater unity among Christians, and their unwillingness to own obstacles to be insurmountable which were once thought to be so. For though the opinions of the learned may be slow to reach the masses, they do so at length, and what is mere scientific belief in one age becomes matter of popular education in the next. And with the increasing pressure of unbelief producing assaults on every form of Christianity, men of what are now different denominations, forced to fight side by side against a common enemy, will, as they are brought to see how much more are the things they have in common than those on which they differ, be likely to feel increasing anxiety to put an end to existing separations.

But, it may be asked, If unity is so desirable, why should not we make a beginning by giving up our Episcopal form of government and accepting that which has been adopted by the majority in Scotland? I will not delay to point out how very short a way towards unity that step would bring us; for we should still have to choose with which of the Presbyterian bodies in Scotland we should join ourselves. When once the breaking of church unity has come to be regarded as a light matter, further splits are likely to take place; and so it has been in this country, on grounds which a stranger, as I am, cannot pretend to understand.

So much as this, however, I know, that some of these divisions have arisen from resistance to supposed encroachments of the State upon the prerogatives of the Church, and from the desire to assert the principle that the Church is no creation of the State, but must, in matters spiritual, hold its own way, whatever kings and parliaments may do. Those who hold that principle ought to be able to appreciate the historical reason for your holding fast to the old constitution of the Church of Scotland. It is within the competence of the State to withdraw privileges from the Church; it may take its property; if it chooses to persecute, it may proscribe the public use of its worship, and make the assembling of its members penal; but to alter the constitution of the Church is outside the province of king or parliament. What took place in Scotland in the reign of William III., has had its parallel in Ireland in our own time, though with some differences, characteristic of a modern change of feeling, more tender of the rights of individuals, less alive to the claims of religion. Our Irish Church has been disestablished, and our property taken from us : not, however, with the disregard shown in your case to the sufferings of the existing clergy. On the other hand, in your case, that which the piety of former generations had devoted to the service of God was still, in considerable measure, preserved for religious uses ; but in our case it was actually made a principle that no religious use should be made of our property—a feeling being prevalent in different religious bodies, like that of the harlot in King Solomon's time, of preferring that rather no one should have it, than that it should pass into the hands of a rival. But all these arrangements relate to secular matters. But suppose that Parliament had interfered with us in spiritual matters ; suppose it had decreed that we should give up our Episcopal form of government, I am sure that men of all religions, and men of no religion, would allow that we should be right in considering such a decree as outside the competence of Parliament, and treating it with complete disregard. This was precisely the feeling of your clergy in the days of William III. The spoiling of their worldly goods they submitted to ; but the alteration by the State of the constitution of the Church they regarded as null and void.

But undoubtedly the repressive measures used had the effect of diminishing the numbers of the Church, and reducing its adherents for a time to what was then a very small minority, and still is a minority of the nation.

Yet before you yield to the temptation of joining the larger number, look outside your own portion of this island, and see what a price you would have to pay, in the hope of gaining greater unity at home, by losing unity with that great body, whose ramifications are spread over all the civilised world, and of which you now boast to be a component part. If it be theoretically within the power of the Church to alter its form of government, yet that which is the common heritage of all ought not to be changed without the assent of all, nor without grave and weighty reasons.

Are there such reasons for parting with the Apostolic form of Church government? Is it the case that that form of government by single persons, which was natural in the days of Imperial Rome, has proved itself unsuited to our democratic times? Experience has proved the contrary; there never was a time when the institution was more vigorous and more successful than at present. Our generation has seen the foundation of a number of Sees, both missionary and colonial; and it has been found that with the gain of fresh and active leaders, Church life has taken new and vigorous growth. It must be remembered that these new Sees have all been founded by voluntary effort; and since people are not fond of giving money where they get no adequate return, the fact that the stream of contributions for this purpose has not ceased to flow, shows that the donors are persuaded that what has been already devoted to this object has been well expended. I saw lately that what has been raised for the increase of the home Episcopate in England within the last few years exceeds £450,000.[1] And I can add testimony from Ireland. Since our disestablishment and disendowment, we are a poor Church, and have no money to throw away on needless luxuries. Yet this last year has witnessed the restoration and re-endowment, by voluntary effort, of one of ten Sees suppressed fifty years ago (Clogher). It is true that with the facilities of communication which the railroad system affords, a bishop can now take charge of a larger district than in former times, and therefore that a smaller number of bishops than in former days might well suffice us. But in this particular case there was a large population of Church people who complained that under former arrangements they had not enjoyed adequate Episcopal supervision, and who were eager to have a bishop of their own. And they gave such practical proof of their eagerness by contributions for the purpose, that it was not possible to refuse to accede to their wishes.

There is nothing to wonder at in the advantages which experience shows attend our form of Church government. No matter how democratic a society may be, it must have its leaders ; and it always is when powerful men come to the front that the society makes progress. Presbyterianism in Scotland has had its leaders, several of whom — such as Chalmers, Guthrie, Macleod, Tulloch — have made their names known outside their own communion, and outside their own country. I suppose no bishop ever exercised more power than such a man as Chalmers exercised. The only difference, then, in

---

[1] The sum raised by voluntary effort for the endowment of seven new English Sees is now (1899) close on £540,000.

our system is, that those who lead are given an official right to lead. It is, after all, comparatively few who can push themselves to the front by force of character, and can acquire the submission of their equals in rank by great superiority of natural gifts. Many a man, too, though competent for a higher post, yet, when the charge of a single church has been committed to him as his proper duty, feels that it would be presumption in him to undertake the charge of all the churches, and that in thus stepping out of his sphere he would be likely to neglect the work that specially belonged to him. And yet such a man, when duly commissioned to undertake the larger oversight, and aided by the loyal co-operation of his former brethren, who now own him as a spiritual father, has often been found to be a more valuable guide and counsellor than men of more pushing nature and more brilliant powers.

Your late Bishop I had the honour of counting among my personal friends. I had known him by his University reputation, and by some of his published writings, when he paid us a visit in Ireland, and won for himself many friends by his mild and genial good sense. It is no light undertaking to succeed him, and to assume the responsibility of being one of the leaders of your Church along the paths which, in the unknown future, stretch before us. We are told that in the case of Timothy there were prophecies which went before to guide the Ephesian Church in their choice of a leader. We have now no such inspired guidance, and can only be directed in our choice by those indications of fitness which a previous career has afforded.

In the case of him whom you have chosen, a long and intimate acquaintance would enable me to speak of such auguries of success, if it were not that I prefer to speak of something better: I mean the gift which we are about to supplicate God's Spirit to grant, and which we doubt not will be bestowed by Him who is ever more ready to give than we to ask. When we read of the gift of God that was in Timothy by the laying on of hands, we might imagine that miraculous powers were spoken of. Yet surely when Timothy is directed to neglect not the gift that was in him, to stir it up, we cannot imagine that what was intended was that he was not to allow miraculous powers to decay for want of exercise. It is clear that the gift here spoken of was not one peculiar to one age of the Church, but one which is still bestowed in answer to believing prayer. I care not, therefore, to form an estimate of the human powers of the instrument with which God's work is to be done in this diocese. I look to Him through whose might weakness can be made strong. I doubt not that in answer to your prayers that very same gift which was bestowed on Timothy will rest on him who, by the laying on of hands, is to be entrusted with the superintendence of this Church; and if he doubts, as he well may, his own sufficiency for the task imposed on him, he may be assured that God's grace bestowed on him will not be in vain. One thought is enough to banish either timidity at the outset, or elation in success, or despondency at apparent failure—"Not I, but the grace of God which is with me."

SERMON XVII

DIOTREPHES

"I wrote unto the Church : but Diotrephes, who loveth to have the pre-eminence among them, receiveth us not. Wherefore, if I come, I will remember his deeds which he doeth, prating against us with malicious words : and not content therewith, neither doth he himself receive the brethren, and forbiddeth them that would, and casteth them out of the Church.—3 John, 9, 10.

As there is evidence that there were apostolic letters which have not come down to us, it might be supposed that, since only a selection of apostolic letters remains to us, what would have been preserved for the instruction of the Church universal would be those letters which were addressed to Churches ; and that letters written to private persons would have been allowed to perish, as being only interesting to those to whom they were addressed. There would seem to have been a tendency towards some such principle of selection. We have reason to think that some early copyists of the Epistle to the Romans did not think it worth their while to transcribe the list of names which fills so much of the last chapter—a list which perhaps we may not think of peculiar edification for us, though, no doubt, to those to whom it was first written, the

mention of themselves by name must have been
perhaps the most interesting part of the whole letter ;
and though that list supplies much information as
to the history of the early Church, as well as some
lessons for our own instruction, on which I have
not now time to dwell. There seem also to have
been in circulation copies of St John's First Epistle
not accompanied by the Second and Third, although,
no one can read the three without feeling that all
are the work of the same author, and though we
have second-century testimony to the genuineness
of the two smaller. The private letters were no
doubt thought by the copyists to contain matter
not needful for the knowledge of the whole Church.
But we have every reason to bless God's Providence
which has directed that we should have kept for
our instruction specimens of the apostles' private
intercourse with their converts, as well as of their
public teaching. The letter of Paul to Philemon,
for example, though as completely private a letter
as any can be—being written merely to bespeak a
master's favourable reception for a repentant run-
away slave—not only throws a flood of light on the
character of the apostle, but also, by its unmistak-
able marks of genuineness, has been of the greatest
use in dispelling doubts as to the genuineness of
the companion Epistle to the Colossians.

And in general it may be said that the stability
of the documents on which our faith rests is exactly
proportioned to the abundance of local and personal
details which account for the human origin of the
composition. It is exactly because Paul's Epistles
are so rich in such details, because the human

element in them is so prominent, that their authority
is so unshakable.   There are some of them whose
genuineness the most sceptical critics have not
ventured to impugn ; and while the Gospels, whose
writers are silent about themselves, have been set
down as legendary narratives of a later generation,
these Pauline Epistles are recognised by every one
as contemporary records of what Christ's first
disciples thought and believed concerning their
Master.

It is for the want of such details that the body of
writings, of which the letter whence I have taken the
text is one, have been exposed to peculiar assaults.
Internal evidence proves that the Gospel and the
three Epistles are the work of the same author,
but these writings say nothing as to his own history.
The name of the apostle John is not once named
in them.   Very early tradition, however, connects
them with that apostle's name.   This much we may
say is historically certain : that, at the end of the
first century, or the beginning of the second, there
lived in Asia Minor a man of high repute in the
Christian community, whose name was John, who
was generally known as "the elder," and who was
looked on as having been a personal companion
of our Saviour, or, at least, as able to give peculiarly
trustworthy information as to the incidents of His
life and the history of His first disciples.   It is very
natural to think that this elder must have been the
author of the Epistle from which I have taken the
text, where he gives himself the name of "the elder."
Whether or not he was the same as the apostle
John, is a point which has been disputed.   The

earliest witnesses identify them without a doubt.
But when the age of literary criticism began, one
or two distinguished names in early times, and a
very large body of modern critics, including some
of undoubted orthodoxy, have maintained the opinion
that there were in Asia Minor two Johns. Indeed
some of the bolder of the destructive school now
fall back on the older opinion that there was but
one John at Ephesus; only that, according to them,
this was not the apostle, who, they think, was never
out of Palestine.

It is interesting to examine whether the traditional
account of the origin of these letters receives any
confirmation or the reverse from the personal notices
contained in the Third Epistle, the only one of the
three which enters into any personal details. This
does bear on the face of it the marks of being an
occasional composition, and it gives a very intelligible history of the circumstances under which it
was written. The writer says, in the 9th verse, that
he had "written somewhat to the Church,"—the
Church doubtless of which Gaius, the person
addressed, was a member. The phrase ἔγραψά τι
rather suggests that the letter in question was not
a very long one; and it seems to me not an im-
probable conjecture that we have that letter still
in the Second Epistle, that " to the elect lady," by
which expression many have thought that a Church,
not an individual, is intended. It appears that the
bearers of this letter met with very varied reception
from the different members of the Church to which
they came. Some, of whom Gaius was one, received
them hospitably and cordially; but from others

chief of whom Diotrephes is named, they not only got no welcome but were violently opposed. The question whether or not they should be entertained, actually made a schism in the Church. When the missionaries return to him by whom they had been sent, and give an account of their journey, he writes this short letter, of praise and thanks to Gaius for his hospitality and kindness, of censure on those who had taken an opposite course, and promising a speedy visit from himself. There is nothing else touched on in the letter—which has no marks of having been written with the purpose of commending any dogmatic views. For though questions of doctrine are treated of largely in the First Epistle, and referred to in the Second, in this the only controversy alluded to is on a question of Church government.

The letter, then, may be pronounced to have the highest marks of genuineness. It is quite intelligible if we accept its own account of its origin, and it is difficult to invent any other. We cannot conceive any object which a forger could have in concocting a letter which brings out no other point than that the writer to whom it is ascribed, and whose authority it would be the forger's interest to exalt, was regarded with distrust and hostility by some Churches in his own lifetime. We know well that it is a mistake to imagine that the Church of the apostles' days was quite free from heresy and schism. We know from Paul's Epistles that those evils which have so rent the later Church as to make some doubt of her divine mission, existed in it from the first ; that even in the days of the Church's inspired teachers, false doctrine widely prevailed among nominal members of the Church; that there were even then parties which divided the Church, calling themselves after the name of this or that one of the preachers of the Gospel. There is then nothing in the slightest degree incredible in the statement that the apostle John's authority was not universally admitted, and that some members of the Church set themselves in opposition to him. But however likely that such a state of things may have existed, it is not the less unlikely that a forger would represent it as existing. Prone as men always have been to believe that former times were better than their own, it is not likely that he would himself have believed that such could have been the palmy days of the Church; and if he had believed it, it would still be his interest to be silent as to anything disparaging the authority of the teacher in whose name he wrote.

Regarding then this letter as a fragment out of the real life of the later apostolic Church, let us try to understand the state of things which it reveals. And in the first place observe how much is implied in the fact that a controversy should have arisen concerning the exercise of hospitality—for this was, one may say, the favourite Christian virtue.

Whoever joined the Christian Community became one of a real brotherhood, the ties of which knew no limitation of race or country. Thenceforward no land was to him a foreign country. Wherever he went he found friends and brothers, and, especially if he travelled, labouring for his Master's cause, their houses were open to him, and they supplied him with all things needful. A number of New Testament Texts will start to your recollection in which you have other examples of this hospitality and exhortations to practise it. You will remember that, on Lydia's conversion, this was the test by which she claimed to assure herself of the reality of her reception into the company of the faithful: "If ye have judged me to be faithful to the Lord, come into my house and abide there" (Acts xvi. 15). You will remember that one of the qualifications for the office of a bishop, as enumerated in the Epistles to Timothy and to Titus, is, that he must be "a man given to hospitality" (1 Tim. iii.; Titus i. 8). You will remember that it is directed that a woman shall be taken into the number of the Church's widows, "if she have lodged strangers, if she have washed the saints' feet" (1 Tim. v. 10). You will remember the exhortation of the Epistle to the Hebrews: "Be not forgetful to entertain strangers, for thereby some have entertained angels unawares" (Heb. xiii. 2). And we may gather that this Christian hospitality was sometimes rather heavily taxed, from St Peter's exhortation to afford it cheerfully and with a good grace: "Use hospitality one to another without grudging" (ἄνευ γογγυσμοῦ) (1 Pet. iv. 9). The case in the text then arrests our attention as a singular anomaly in the history of the apostolic Church. It is not, what must have frequently occurred, the case of a cold-hearted, stingy man who, notwithstanding the lessons of Christian love that he had been taught, and which his judgment approved, has not the heart to put them into practice. The error of Diotrephes was one not of practice but of principle.

He is seen inverting the rule that governed Christian conduct elsewhere, making the exercise of hospitality not a duty or a virtue but an offence; not merely not practising it himself, but punishing those who did—"Neither doth he himself receive the brethren, and forbiddeth them that would, and casteth them out of the Church."

It is manifest that it is quite impossible that any Christian could have regarded the exercise of hospitality as a thing in itself deserving of censure. It follows, then, that what was visited with excommunication was the bestowal of hospitality on persons looked on as unworthy of it; on persons, in short, whose presence in the place was judged to be opposed to the welfare of the Church.

In the Second Epistle ascribed to John, the writer himself had treated as a sin the exercise of hospitality to the enemies of the Church: "If there come any unto you and bring not this doctrine, receive him not into your house, neither bid him God speed: for he that biddeth him God speed is partaker of his evil deeds." But while in the Second Epistle it is corruption of doctrine that is spoken of as disqualifying a man from sharing in the hospitality of the Christian community, there is no hint given in the Third Epistle of any divergence of doctrinal teaching. The conduct of Diotrephes is ascribed to resentment at a supposed infringement of his personal rights of precedence. There seems, then, but one explanation of the facts elicited from the letter. The messengers of John, when they came in the character of apostolic legates to the Church to which they had been sent, find themselves confronted

seem to be antecedent to that apostle; and we
gather that before his arrival in Asia Minor this
form of government, whether instituted by St Paul,
or developed by spontaneous growth, had already
established itself. Whatever may have been its
origin, the letters to the seven Churches in the Book
of Revelation, as well as historical tradition, lead us
to believe that the apostle John gave it his subsequent sanction.

Internal evidence, then, has led us to the conclusion that the group of writings, of which the Epistle
we have been considering is one, was written in Asia
Minor by one who claimed patriarchal authority over
the Churches of the district. The only question
that seems to me historically debatable is, Whether
this was the apostle John or a later person known
as " the elder," to whom this authority had been conceded on the ground of his having seen our Lord
in the flesh ; or else on the ground of such intimate
connection with the apostle John, that he was easily
and early identified with him. As far as the
evidences of our faith are concerned, it does not
much matter how we decide the question. If the
John who wrote the Gospel was an eye-witness and
personal attendant on our Lord, it does not much
matter to us whether or not he was an apostle.
His Gospel would still have as high claims as those
of Mark or Luke, if not higher. But it seems to me
that when so much has been conceded, internal
evidence favours the conclusion that the opinion
which has always prevailed in the Church is correct—
that the apostle was the writer. Even in the letter
we are considering, the writer's claims to authority

are taken for granted rather than insisted on as a
matter open to serious dispute. He treats as idle
talk (φλναρῶν, is the word used) the objections that
had been raised against his claims. When we take
in connection with the Epistles the Gospel which
is certainly the work of the same author, we find
the same phenomenon—a taking for granted of claims
which it seems to be thought needless to assert
directly. It is not directly said that the author of
the Gospel is the apostle John, or even the disciple
whom Jesus loved. But every one who has read
the Gospel from the earliest times has inferred from
it that that unnamed disciple was the author. I
have already elsewhere referred to the singular fact,
which has been observed, that a person who had no
other than the fourth Gospel would never discover
that there was an apostle of the name of John.
Even when our Lord's forerunner is spoken of, he
is not, as in the other Gospels, given the distinctive
title of the Baptist, but is called simply John, as if
there were no other John from whom it was necessary
to distinguish him. This is intelligible enough if the
apostle were the author of the Gospel, for he would
be exactly the person who would never in speaking
of the Baptist have felt any necessity to avoid con-
fusion by giving him a distinctive title ; but if any one
else were the author, it is not conceivable that so
distinguished an apostle should have been passed
over in silence ; still less so if the writer had planned
what has come to pass, namely, that his composition
should be regarded as that apostle's work.

Before I conclude I ought, perhaps, to say something on a question suggested by the discussion in

which we have engaged. According to the view I have taken, Diotrephes erred through excess of zeal in maintaining the rights of a local Church and of himself as its officer. Now the rights of local Churches are what controversy has forced us to be earnest in maintaining. We have been forced to resist foreign usurpations, and one of the Thirty-nine Articles which our clergy subscribe, denies to the Bishop of Rome, or any external bishop, any jurisdiction in this realm. The controversy of which I speak existed before the Reformation. In the time of Henry VIII., the denial of foreign jurisdiction was made by men who afterwards proved their attachment to the system of doctrine which we call Romish. The controversy has existed in the unreformed Church down to our own time, and the party now prevalent in the Roman Church look on Nationalism as an enemy not less dangerous than Protestantism, if indeed it be distinct from it. The question then arises, What rights have local Churches against the Church universal? What power have they of lawfully resisting an authority which claims to speak in the name of the universal Church? This is a point on which we must be careful against making rash assertions, or taking ground which we shall not be able to maintain. The advocates of Rome find their task most agreeably lightened if, instead of having to prove their own doctrine that their bishop has by divine right authority over other Churches, they can be allowed to content themselves with overthrowing the opposite doctrine, that every national Church is by divine right independent of every other. If this were true, we should at once have to settle what is a national Church. In the time of the Roman Empire were all the nations united under one civil government bound by Christ's law to constitute a single Church? In the time of the Heptarchy might there have been seven national Churches in England, and a national Church for each province in Ireland? or, now that we are united under one civil government, is it wrong to have more than one Church for England, Ireland, and Scotland? or is every island entitled to have a Church of its own? And if so, how big an island? Is it essential that there should be a separate Church for Guernsey, Jersey, Alderney, or Sark? Plainly, the Word of God defines none of these things any more than it defines the political limits of nations. It merely teaches in general terms the duty of submission to constituted authority, and the sin of causelessly disturbing lawful order. But there is no divine right either of independence or of submission. The Bishop of Rome has by divine right no authority over the Church of England, any more than the people of England have by divine right authority over India. But it is no more contrary to God's Word that His Church should develop itself in a form in which the Bishop of Rome should have authority in England, than it is that the Bishop of Winchester should be Diocesan of Guernsey, or the Archbishop of Canterbury Metropolitan of Australia.

For just cause, however, existing ecclesiastical, as well as civil, relations may be changed. There was just cause why, in the time of Henry VIII., the Church of England resolved that it would be no longer subject to Rome, far stronger than there was when the Americans resolved they would no longer be politically subject to England. For the claim of Roman supremacy had been originally established by fraud and imposture, it had been falsely asserted to exist by divine right, and when the Roman title-deeds were discovered to be forged, there was nothing in the manner in which its power had been exercised to lead men to excuse the badness of its foundation. The Roman power had long ceased to be exercised for the benefit of its subjects, and had become a selfish and grinding tyranny. Those, however, who cast off the yoke of Rome, protested that they had no desire to separate from the universal Church, and it was a common thing to appeal from the Pope's sentence to that of a future Council freely assembled.

In the early Church, though there was very considerable diversity of local usage, that diversity was restrained within certain limits; and, to mention one well-known controversy, those who incurred suspicion of Judaizing tendency by conforming in their Paschal celebrations to Jewish usage rather than to the custom of the Christian Church, were forced to give up their peculiarities, on the pain of losing friendly intercourse with their brethren. The same duty of brotherly union which forbids the Christians of any one place to put themselves in schismatic isolation from the members of the Church of that place, would also forbid the members of a local Church from wantonly severing themselves from the rest. And though there are doctrinal truths which we could not surrender to any human authority, yet in matters of ritual and practice a particular

Church would not be right in resisting the voice of the universal Church if she had any organ for uttering it.

There now is no such acknowledged organ. Our own Church has full power to make ordinances for itself, and none of her members would be justified in disobeying these ordinances on the ground of their differing from what had been ordained elsewhere. Yet a Church must not abuse this its rightful liberty, nor would it act wisely were it to make ordinances in total disregard of what has been done at other times and in other places. In our individual conduct we should resist any attempt of our neighbours to interfere with that liberty of action to which we are entitled. Yet we are not indifferent to the good opinion of others whom we respect, and we are glad when the use we make of our liberty commends itself to the approbation of wise and good men. Even in such a trifling matter as dress, we do not use the liberty which the law gives us of attiring ourselves in any manner we please within the limits of decency. We conform to what is usual in our country and in the rank of life to which we belong; and there is no doubt that a man would do himself a real injury if he were to set the prejudices of his neighbours at defiance. Others would set him down as vain, odd, wilful, fond of singularity, and so forth, and in this way there might take place real diminution of his influence in serious matters. A local Church, then, in like manner, even when deciding on matters on which neighbouring Churches have no legal right to in‑ terfere, cannot afford wholly to disregard their opinion. And the great intercourse which modern facilities of travel produce between peoples of different lands, makes it desirable that there should be no unnecessary differences of usage to obstruct the freedom of mutual communion — nothing to prevent those who agree in faith from joining in common worship. It is to be hoped that our Church, claiming and possessing as she does the right to make rules for herself independent of external dictation, will yet always use her liberty in such a way that her decisions will carry with them the sympathy and approval of dispassionate judges elsewhere.

SERMON XVIII

FASTS AND FEASTS [1]

"Hungry and thirsty their soul fainted in them: then they cried unto the Lord in their trouble, and He delivered them out of their distress."—PSALM cvii. 5, 6.

THE two verses I have read form the recurring burden of this 107th Psalm. It describes successively men tried with various forms of distress, and when at their wits' end for trouble, crying to the Lord, and obtaining from Him deliverance. A couple of other Psalms, the 78th and the 106th, deal with the same theme, only bringing out more strongly the points of men's forgetfulness of God in times when there is no trouble, and the transient impression that deliverance makes on them: "when He slew them then they sought Him; and they returned and enquired early after God, and they remembered that God was their rock and the High God their Redeemer. Nevertheless, they did but flatter Him with their mouth, and they lied unto Him with their tongue" (Ps. lxxviii. 34). And it is true that when danger threatens, and other help there is none, the heart of the least religious turns naturally to prayer to

[1] Preached in Trinity College Chapel on Christmas Day, 1895.

God, if perchance from Him succour can be gained. Stories are told, of which some may possibly be true, of atheists in danger of shipwreck, dinning with supplications and vows the God whose existence they had denied. Thus, religion has come with many to be looked on as a thing suitable for times of distress, anxiety, sickness; and thoughts of God to be regarded as well postponed till the hour of death; nor even admitted then, if some kindly attendant should cheer the dying sinner with the suggestion that it is too soon for so dismal a topic yet.

Our Lord compared the men of His generation to wayward children whom it was impossible to satisfy, who rejected John the Baptist because he lived an ascetic life unlike that of ordinary men, and yet were as unwilling to acknowledge the claim of our Lord Himself to be the bearer of a message from God, because they saw Him not different from other men in habits of life, mixing freely with ordinary society, and not unwilling to take part in their merrymaking and their feasts. I think this perverseness (something like which may be seen at the present day), is to be accounted for by the prevalence of the habit of mind of which I have been speaking, of regarding religion as a guest too solemn to be made one's daily companion, and only to be sought if need arise of a deliverer or a consoler. John the Baptist, clad in prophetic garb, and disdaining usual enjoyments, could easily be recognised as a fitting representative of religion; but however welcome the appearance to men whose sin-burdened consciences made them prepared to believe in a prophecy of wrath to come and eager to learn means of escape, those who lived at ease in the world, with whom all things went well, resented the intrusion on their tranquillity by so startling a visitor. With our Lord, on the other hand, the difficulty was to recognise in one of so everyday an aspect, a title to speak in the name of religion. How should one whose mode of life differed nothing from that of other men, assume the claims of a prophet, and presume to instruct and admonish doctors far better instructed in the law than He?

It might be supposed from what I have said, that I adopted the ancient theory that fear was the mother of religion, and that men were only led to invoke the Deity because they conceived of Him as a Being having the forces of nature at His command, and thus so well able either to do us injury or to protect us from it, that it would be foolhardy to neglect to propitiate Him. It is pleasant that history obliges us to take a view more honourable to human nature ; for some of the earliest religious celebrations we know of, had their origin not in fear, but in the joyous gladness of gratitude. All mankind, and indeed the greater part of living creatures, are constrained to live—not indeed from day to day, but from year to year. It has been said that London is always within a week of starvation ; by which I suppose is meant that there is not more than a week's consumption in all the food contained in the city. It might be said in the same way that the world is always within a year of starvation. Each year's harvest produces on an average but a little more than one year's supply of food. We have no experience of such a thing as a total and absolute failure of all crops throughout the kingdom, but even a deficient harvest means penury and privation to a great many, and would be still more fatal if it were not that the shortcomings of one place are supplied by the abundance of another. But if we could imagine such a thing as that for a single year nature's annual bounty were denied all over the world, how few of earth's inhabitants would be found in existence at the end? And though God's goodness has ordained that while the earth remaineth, seed-time and harvest shall not cease, yet in any one place there is enough of uncertainty to keep up the anxiety of the husbandman. Scorching drought may withhold the moisture without which the herbage cannot sprout; drenching rains may intercept the ripening influence of the sun, or torrents sweep the fertile soil away; winds may prostrate his standing corn, or hurricanes tear it up and scatter it abroad; devastating hail may wreck his vineyards, or insect hordes may appropriate to themselves the fruits of his toil. There are so many risks of failure from causes beyond human power to control, that a weight of anxiety is lifted from the husbandman's mind when all peril is over and the harvest safely gathered in. Hence, from the earliest times, harvest-time has been proverbially associated with rejoicing. You will remember the verse from Isaiah which we read in the lesson to-day: "They joy before Thee according to the joy in harvest."

But what I wish to point out is, that as far back as history reaches, these harvest rejoicings were always connected with religion, being partly expressions of gratitude to the unseen Bestower of the bounty received, mingled, no doubt, with hope that by making Him propitious there would be gained security for the bestowal of like benefit another year.

The three great religious feasts of the Jews were each connected with a harvest ; and let me say, in passing, that the very phrase "religious feast" bears testimony to the connection of religion with times of merrymaking. The three feasts are described in Exodus as the Feast of Unleavened Bread, the Feast of Harvest, and the Feast of Ingathering, "when thou hast gathered in all thy labours at the end of the year." The names of the two latter feasts speak for themselves. The Feast of Unleavened Bread, though like the others a feast of thanksgiving, was, no doubt, in its chief intent thanksgiving for a different benefit, namely, the deliverance of the nation from Egyptian bondage; but it, too, was connected with thanksgiving for harvest blessings. It synchronized with the first reception of the fruits of the earth, the beginning of barley harvest ; then it was enjoined that before any one ate green ears or parched corn or bread, a sheaf of the first fruits should be brought in to be presented to God ; and from that presentation were to be counted the seven weeks which were to pass before the celebration of the completed harvest. These harvest celebrations were no peculiarity of the Jewish nation. Many of you will remember the rustic dances which Virgil inculcates as a religious duty on the husbandman before he puts his sickle into the corn ; but it is more striking to call to mind what corresponded to the Jewish feast of Ingathering, celebrated at the conclusion of the vintage, those vintage feasts concerning which legend had so much to tell, and to which we certainly owe the Grecian drama.

taken away "—surely we have not said all when we own that it is but a loan we are required to give back. Have we not cause to ask ourselves : Has the Lord taken away all that the Lord gave? In comparison of the loss, no doubt, what is left seems for the moment insignificant. Yet, in truth, it is not so. Few are so unhappy as to be bereft of all earthly love, and a moment ago I referred to the alchemy by which love and trust can transform the darkest and heaviest load of sorrow into precious treasure. And if earthly stay there be none, cannot Faith reveal in Him who sends the trial, One still more worthy of love and trust, One who does not afflict willingly, who, if He leads us through fire and through water, will bring us out into a wealthy place?

If we are to have this support in time of trial, it is not then first we are to begin to seek it ; not then first we are to begin to know our God as our Father and our Friend. Can we know Him as such if we habitually regard Him as a stranger—a physician who may be called into the house when our own skill does not suffice to find a remedy—or a neighbour whom politeness induces us to ask in to fill the table on some occasion of unusual festivity? If we have learned habitually to feel His presence, we need no special thoughts for feast days and for days of humiliation. We have not then to turn our eyes in some new direction, but only to fix them more earnestly on the object towards which we had been always looking.

If the sense of His goodness teaches us to ask ourselves, What shall we render unto the Lord for all His benefits, conscious as we are that no tribute of

ours can add aught to His Majesty, Christ has
taught us how to show our love to Him by love to
our brethren whom He is not ashamed to call *His*
brethren. "This commandment have we from Him,"
said His apostle, "that he who loveth God love his
brother also." Even before His coming, the Jewish
prophets had pointed out the spirit in which both
fasts and feasts should be kept. "Is this the fast I
have chosen," said Isaiah, "the day for a man to
afflict his soul; to bow down his head as a bulrush,
and to spread sackcloth and ashes under him; wilt
thou call this a fast, and an acceptable day to the
Lord? Is not this the fast that I have chosen? To
loose the bands of wickedness, to undo the bands of
the yoke, and to let the oppressed go free and that
ye break every yoke? Is it not to deal thy bread to
the hungry, and that thou bring the poor that are cast
out to thy house? When thou seest the naked that
thou cover him, and that thou hide not thyself from
thine own flesh." And with regard to feasts we have
in the book of Esther an exact description of a feast
celebrated in the same way as that in which we are
accustomed to keep the feast of to-day: "A good day,
a day of feasting and gladness, of sending portions
one to another, and of gifts to the poor."

No religion has done what ours has done in binding
together the service of man and the service of
God; and the prominence of this feature of our
religion was, beyond doubt, designedly given it by
its Founder, who lost no opportunity of connecting
together our duty to God and our duty to man. If
fear of threatened evil suggests a consciousness of
ill desert and a need to propitiate a justly offended

God, which finds its natural expression in humiliation and fasting, Christ has not merely emphasized the Old Testament teaching that God is merciful and gracious, long-suffering, forgiving iniquity, transgression, and sin ; but He has pointed out that our duty to God, of seeking His forgiveness of our offences, carries with it the duty to man of granting forgiveness to those who have offended us. He not only pointed out the connection of these duties in His discourses ; He printed it on the minds of His followers in a striking parable, and He made them include an acknowledgment of it in their daily prayers. And the lesson was so well taught to all His disciples, that an apostle who had not personally been His hearer, was able to repeat it : " Be ye kind one to another, tender-hearted, forgiving one another even as God, for Christ's sake, hath forgiven you."

And so likewise with feasts, in which we gratefully acknowledge God's bounty towards us. Our Lord linked with that acknowledgment the obligation of imitating towards our brethren the bounty of our Heavenly Father : " Freely ye have received," He said, " freely give." And He taught that our giving was not to be checked by the unworthiness or the ingratitude of those whom it may be our duty to benefit, if we are to be children of the Highest who makes His sun to shine on the evil and the good, and is kind to the unthankful and to the evil.

Those who imagine that religion must be a gloomy thing ought to recognise that of our religion joy is the key-note. " Rejoice in the Lord alway," was the apostle's direction. In our Church system feasts predominate over fasts. The fifty days of Pentecostal joy predominate over the Lenten fast, which, though it ultimately swelled to forty days, was, when first we hear of it, limited to the interval between our Lord's death and resurrection, variously counted as one day, or two days, or forty hours.

The feast we celebrate to-day commemorates the angelic announcement: "Behold I bring you good tidings of great joy." It is a feast not prompted like the feasts of old by gratitude at the reception of the bounty of nature, but is held when nature at her sternest locks up her stores ; so that its celebration is not of a secular feast springing out of gladness for temporal benefits, and artificially made to assume a religious aspect, but is essentially of a religious feast springing out of gratitude for the greatest of all spiritual benefits. It only assumes a secular aspect because, by our Lord's own ordinance, our gladness for mercy shown to ourselves is made to diffuse itself by conferring good on those whom it is in our power to benefit. And since it was His work, not to found a philosophy as an instrument of solitary self-culture, but a Church whose members should be bound together by mutual love, so this commemorative feast to which I bid you now is not merely, as many too exclusively regard it, a means of grace by which our own souls are fed, but a means of drawing us into closer union with our brethren in Christ, the assemblage of whom, no less than that which is given us in this holy rite, is called the Lord's Body.

SERMON XIX

THE CHRISTIAN'S PEACE

"The same day at evening . . . came Jesus and stood in the midst, and saith unto them, 'Peace be unto you.'"
—JOHN xx. 19.

ONE of the few remains of very early Christian antiquity is a work written about the end of the second century, which professes to give a report of discourses delivered on a missionary tour by the apostle Peter. It cannot be described as orthodox, being in fact tainted with Ebionite heresy, but it is valuable as recording for us the opinions and practices of some of those half-converted Jewish sects which combined an acknowledgment of at least the Divine Mission of Jesus with an attempt to propagate peculiar opinions of their own under cover of the authority of our Lord or of His original apostles. The reason why I cite the book now is that it describes Peter as, at the commencement of every address to the heathen crowds which flocked about him, first saluting them in "the accustomed manner," the "pious manner," "the manner prescribed by religion." If we enquire what these vague descriptions are intended to denote, there can be little doubt that the salutation was that which in

the text, and in two other verses which follow soon
after in the same chapter, the risen Lord is related to
have used : " Peace be unto you." He is represented
as using the same salutation on this occasion in the
earlier account given in the last chapter of St Luke's
Gospel. There are many traces that the fourth
evangelist was acquainted with St Luke's Gospel,
but it should be mentioned that although this salutation is found in St Luke's text, as given in all the
most ancient Greek MSS., it is not found in some
early Latin translations. How this is to be accounted
for is a subject for discussion by critical editors, with
which it would be irrelevant now to occupy you.

It matters less to enquire what amount of confirmation St John's narrative receives from other
evangelists, because this whole 20th chapter of St
John receives independent confirmation from the
immemorial usage of the Church. For example,
knowing as we do that in the beginning of our
religion Christianity bore to heathen outsiders the
character of a Jewish sect, it must have been then
surprising, and seems still to call for explanation,
that this Jewish sect should have been without what
even heathens knew to be one of the most prominent
characteristics of Judaism, viz., the Saturday observance. Even from those portions of the works of
Latin writers which we commonly read in our own
university studies, we learn that the Jews were known
to the Romans as a circumcised people, and as
observers of the Sabbath ; and the word Sabbath
then had the meaning which it still retains in
some European languages, and was exclusively
appropriated to the seventh day of the week. There

was indeed at the beginning of Christianity a controversy whether Gentile Christians ought not of necessity to be circumcised. We know that there was from the Acts of the Apostles, and from two of Paul's Epistles; but the dispute was settled during Paul's lifetime, and is not referred to as still alive in his later Epistles. It was decided that circumcision should be treated as a thing indifferent—a national custom which men of Jewish birth might observe if they chose, but which Gentiles might disregard without reproach; and since after the destruction of Jerusalem the Gentile section of the Church predominated immensely over the Jewish, the idea that a Christian ought of necessity to be circumcised disappears from Church history.

The controversy concerning Sabbath observance excited far less stir, and is not mentioned in the Acts, but we know from two of Paul's Epistles that it existed, and was decided on the same principles of mutual toleration. The Jew was not to be blamed for regarding the day, since he regarded it to the Lord, and the Gentile who did not comply with this national usage was not to be judged in respect of the Sabbath. But while the observance of the Saturday thus fell into the background, the usage of holding the Christian meetings for worship on the Sundays dates from apostolic times. I need not quote so late an authority as Justin Martyr, the earliest of uninspired writers who gives us information as to the details of early Christian ritual; for we know both from the Acts and from Paul's Epistles that Sunday was the day of the Christian weekly services. We may well believe that an institution which we can trace to so

early a date must have been of apostolic appointment. Yet those who are not satisfied with ordinary
historical evidence, and will accept no Church ordinance without Scripture warrant for it, would be
puzzled to find any for this transfer to the first day
of the week, of the dignity once conferred on the
seventh. We are at no loss to understand why this
honour should be given to that which, according to
all the evangelists, was the day of our Lord's resurrection ; and since the observance of the Lord's
Day can be traced back to a date before any of our
Gospels was written, we have in this point of primitive ritual the earliest of all testimonies to the fact,
that the belief of the Christian Church from the very
first was that their Lord rose again from the dead on
that day. But on the connection of this day with
religious assembling, we get most light from this
20th chapter of St John, whence we learn that our
Lord not only appeared to the assembled disciples on
the evening of the resurrection day, but on that day
week He found them assembled again, and it is
natural to believe that it was this manifestation of
Himself on two successive Sundays, to a meeting of
collected disciples, which suggested to the Church the
practice of assembling on that day.

Now, just as the statement of St John xx. that our
Lord appeared to His disciples on two succeeding
Sundays receives independent confirmation from the
habitual usage of the Church in honouring that day of the
week, so in like manner does the statement of the same
chapter, that on these occasions our Lord commenced
the manifestation of His presence with the salutation,
"Peace be unto you." I have already spoken of the

testimony borne by the Jewish section of the Church, and if it be objected that this was but an ordinary Eastern salutation (as can be shown from passages in the Old Testament), which has continued in use in the same countries down to our own day, I must point out that in the uncanonical authority which I have cited, it is represented, not as a form of secular courtesy, but of pious and religious usage. However, the use of this salutation was not confined to one section, but obtained such prominence in universal liturgical usage, that we are well disposed to receive the account of this practice given by Cyril of Alexandria, namely, that our Lord by His own use of it imposed it as a kind of law on the children of the Church. We find from St Chrysostom that the salutation was then used four times in the service. The bishop on entering the Church addressed the congregation with, " Peace be unto you." There is by no means uniformity among ourselves as to the prefatory words suitable for beginning a sermon, but at the time of which I speak the bishop began with, " Peace be unto you." There was a previous salutation of Mercy and Peace at the end of the reading, and the closing dismissal was also a benediction of Peace. It would carry me too far away from my special subject if I spoke about the kiss of peace, and of the modifications which this apostolic custom received in later practice.

But as for the salutation, " Peace be unto you," I would remark that if it be said that our Lord imposed the use of it as a law on the Church, He did so only by setting the example of using it, and not by having prescribed it as a rule. This may be inferred from the far greater prevalence of this form in the East than in the West. For, naturally, as men went to a greater distance from the apostolic centres, the influence of traditional usage in shaping liturgical practice became more likely to be modified by inferences drawn from the direct study of the Scripture records. So it was (and more in the West than in the East) that the specially Christian salutation, " Peace be unto you," the authority of which in all probability mainly rested on a tradition of apostolic custom, had a powerful rival in the Old Testament salutation which we use ourselves, that of Boaz to his reapers, " The Lord be with you," with the response, " And with thy spirit." In the East, the Christian form seems early to have been, " The grace of the Lord be with you," and I think it likely that both forms are really Apostolic, for you know how in most of his Epistles St Paul combines the two in his opening salutation, " Grace and peace be with you."

It is worth while to quote the use made of this response by St Chrysostom, who draws the attention of the laity to the share they are called vocally to take in the services of the Church, in order to make them feel the duty of making the Church's interests their own. I have no controversial object in citing the opening words of my quotation, for the complete novelty of the practice of withholding the cup from the laity is so universally acknowledged that time need not be spent in producing evidence that it did not exist in Chrysostom's time. He remarks that there are some things in which there is no difference between priest and people. It is not with us as under the old dispensation, when the priests

and the people had not equal rights as to partaking
of holy things, and it was unlawful for the people to
partake of the things in which the priest only had
a right to share. It is not so now, but there is one
body and one cup alike for all. And so also in the
prayers the people have their part. He mentions
then certain prayers in the earlier part of the service
in which the people join vocally. He goes on then
to show that this is also true of that part of the service
which takes place after the uninitiated have with-
drawn. He cites the general confession, in which
then, as now, the people joined audibly ; he cites this
response, "And with thy spirit," in which the people
praying for the priest reciprocate his prayer for them.
Even though the people do not join vocally in
that thanksgiving which even in our language retains
the name of Eucharistic (it being originally very long
and apt to be varied at the discretion of the officia-
ting minister), he shows that the priest is still but
speaking in the name of the people ; for he does not
make the thanksgiving until he has first asked and
obtained the people's assent, he saying, "Let us give
thanks to our Lord God," and they responding, "It is
meet and right so to do." And finally, he says that
it is but a small thing that the people should join
their voices with the priest : for finally they join
them with Cherubim and Seraphim, crying, "Holy,
Holy, Holy, Lord God of Hosts."

And here arises an interesting question. When our
Lord after the Resurrection made this salutation,
"Peace be unto you," did the disciples recognise a
form which He had been constantly in the habit of
using? Strange to say, the records of His life in the

Synoptic Gospels (though we are bound to remember of how small a fragment of His life and teaching they tell us anything) make no mention of His having used this formula, either to the disciples or to the multitude. But we have an account of an earlier sanction given by our Lord to this salutation in that narrative of the instruction given by our Lord to His disciples, when He sent them out two by two, which is reproduced both by St Matthew and St Luke. In this, to use the words of the latter evangelist, he says : " Into whatsoever house ye enter, first say, " Peace be to this house. And if the son of peace be there, your peace shall rest upon it ; if not, it shall turn to you again."

Now, it deserves remark that in those early discourses ascribed to the apostle Peter, he is never represented as using this salutation to his disciples, but only to the mixed multitude of heathen or unconverted Jews who assembled to hear him. It might have been objected, Why give your peace to men who probably may be unworthy of it ? but that objection had been anticipated by our Lord's directions : " Offer your peace to all ; if they be worthy, the gift will remain with them ; if not, it will return to the donors."

It is possible that this practical limitation of the gift of peace to the sons of peace may be indicated in a verse, which I have always been glad that the New Testament revisers did not see their way to alter, notwithstanding the great influence of Westcott and Hort on their committee : I mean the angelic salutation, " Glory to God in the highest, on earth peace, towards men, good will." I daresay there may be some who will sympathise with my conservatism (which, no doubt, is not quite defensible), in feeling that no matter what the manuscript evidence may be, I should dislike to see any change in the words of our English Christmas doxology. But it has to be confessed that in all the Latin speaking section of the Church, the reading is, "Peace to men of good will;" and as this indicates that such was the received reading at the time these Latin translations were made, it is not surprising that it has abundance of confirmation from Greek MSS. I need not discuss whether by "good will" here we are to understand the good disposition of the individual, or, as εὐδοκία so often means, the good pleasure of God; it is enough that the reading with the genitive conveys no different meaning from that conveyed by our Lord's instructions, viz., that the salutation of Peace conveys no effectual benefit if the Son of Peace be not there; for as Isaiah has said, "There is no peace, saith my God, to the wicked."

If we want to know what the salutation of Peace means, we have to reflect a little on its origin. In the security of our modern travel we scarcely realise how much uneasiness was caused in days when there were too many whose hand was against every man, when a company of travellers descried the approach of another band. It would be an anxious question, Are these friends or enemies? Does their coming mean war or peace? And the salutation of peace was a welcome relief of well-grounded apprehensions.[1] It is in this way we can explain most of the Old

---

[1] It seems to me that the reason why our Lord directed His envoys to "salute no man by the way" (Luke x. 4) was in order to preserve the sacred character of their formal official salutation, which was not to be confounded with the ordinary travelling salutation, though it was the same in words.

Testament passages where this salutation is found. Thus, when Joseph's brethren timidly accost Joseph's steward, with excuses for an incident of their former visit which, they feared, exposed them to suspicion, how reassuring was his answer, " Peace be unto you." So, again, when there came to David in the hold, men from Benjamin and Judah, who, he feared, had come to betray him into the hands of his enemies, much needed was their answer of peace : " Thine are we, David, peace, peace be unto thee ; peace be to thy helpers, for God helpeth thee." But most of all was re-assurance necessary when men felt themselves closely brought into the presence of God, who, their consciences told them, for their sins was justly displeased. Thus an angelic vision caused Gideon only alarm, and he cried : " Alas ! O Lord God, because I have seen an angel of the Lord face to face ; " but the Lord said : " Peace be unto thee, fear not ; thou shalt not die." And the same reassuring salutation, " Peace be unto thee ; fear not," was given to Daniel when he fainted at an angelic visitation.

Thus, then, it is intelligible why even if our Lord had not habitually used this salutation in His discourses with His disciples, He should, by anticipation, calm their fears by doing so, when He suddenly manifested Himself to them where the doors were shut ; and it is in- telligible, too, why in the later stories of which I spoke, Peter is represented as commencing thus when address- ing strangers, and not so when addressing friends. And now, is it not a paradox that men who believe that God has, through Christ, proclaimed to them an offer of peace, should anxiously enquire of their friends whether they have found peace, and triumph if they can announce that they have found it themselves? Suppose that a king came with irresistible force against a rebellious city that had fought against him, and, instead of vengeance and punishment, made them a proclamation offering them forgiveness, peace, friendship, alliance, would it not be strange if you found the citizens anxiously enquiring whether they had peace or not? What could you suppose but that they did not believe the proclamation made them, and did not think the king would keep his word. Or else could it be that they did not relish the offer of alliance which the proclamation contained ; and that, knowing though they did, that if they chose to make his enemies theirs, he would fight with them and most surely overcome, yet that in their hearts they preferred to be on the side of his enemies.

If there be any of you here who are troubled with anxiety about your peace, ask yourselves which of these causes is the source of your anxiety. Is it that you do not believe? Is it then so hard to believe that " God so loved the world that He gave His only begotten Son that whosoever believeth in Him should not perish, but have everlasting life." Is it so hard to believe that God loves you—that He desireth not the death of a sinner ? Experience would seem to show that it *is* hard to believe it ; for, with most, their belief in God's power so overmasters any sense they have of His goodness, that they seem unable to attain that perfect love which casteth out fear ; and, not-withstanding all the proofs He has given of His love, are perpetually craving for some assurance that He will not use His power to hurt them—if not in this world, at least in another, where it would seem to be imagined He will have us more completely in His power than He has now.

If your belief in God's power is so great, can you not then believe that if you fight under His banner against sin, the world, and the flesh, He has power to overcome His enemies and yours? For that they are your enemies as well as His, you need not wait for a future life to find out. Those fleshly lusts that war against the soul, war against the body too. The laws of God are written deep in the constitution of the world He has framed; and if it be true that godliness has promise of the life that now is, as well as of that which is to come, it is equally true that the transgression of God's commandments brings punishment here which, though it may be delayed for a time, fails not to be duly exacted. The pleasures of sin are but for a season, and afford no adequate recompense for alliance with a losing cause.

The peace with God which is enjoyed by those who are justified by faith in Christ, does not consist, as some are apt too exclusively to regard it, in release from dismal apprehensions of hell torments. If peace of this kind were all that is to be desired, it is obtained successfully by those who are able to banish from their minds all thoughts of God or of Eternity. There are two attitudes of mind in the presence of danger which are equally contemptible; one, that of the coward who torments himself with ungrounded fears, and allows himself to be paralysed by dread of obstacles which he could easily overcome: the other, that of the presumptuous fool who is bold in rushing into perils because he does not believe in their

passed away, it could scarcely contain many lessons
which we could turn to account in our own practice.
Yet actually the Epistle is one not for one age, but
for every age of the Church.   The apostle rises
above details and lays down general principles which
still admit of constant application.   The section of
the Epistle from which the text is taken has furnished
writers on Christian ethics with lessons on the duties
of a perplexed or an ill-formed conscience, on the
duty of abstaining from acts possibly innocent, but
which our conscience condemns, on the duty of
tenderness to the scruples of others, and for their
sake of sometimes refraining from what we believe
to be innocent, if the unrestrained exercise of our
Christian liberty is likely to be a cause of temptation
to others.

But before saying anything on such topics now,
I wish to dwell a little on the primary application
of the apostle's words, for our feelings and circumstances are so different from those of the persons
to whom the letter was written, that it requires an
effort before we can grasp the historical position.
It is quite necessary to do this in order to be able
properly to appreciate the apostle's advice—advice
which in one age might be only an expression of the
dictates of ordinary good common-sense; in another
age, to the feelings and superstitions of which it may
be quite opposed, might indicate wisdom deserving
of the highest admiration.

Towards understanding, indeed, the feeling of the
Jewish section of his converts, we are helped a good
deal by our knowledge of the caste system of our
Indian Empire.   In India different views have at times

been taken by missionaries as to whether they ought
to tolerate the observance of caste by their converts,
as a mere national custom belonging to the secular
sphere with which religion has no concern, or whether
they should demand of their converts the abandon-
ments of caste on pain of rejection or excommunication.
It is evident the possibility of carrying out the former
plan would depend very much on whether or not
there was any mixture of races in the Church. In
Palestine, in the first age of Christianity, the members
of the Church were all Jews, and there seemed no
reason why they should forsake the Jewish national
customs. They observed the Jewish Sabbaths,
attended the annual feasts, circumcised their children,
went up to the Temple to pray, even taking part in
the offering of the Jewish sacrifices, which after
Christ's coming we should think must to a Christian
have lost all religious significance. By this compliance (if compliance that may be called which was
not so much a concession to the feelings of others
as a satisfaction to the feelings and prejudices in
which themselves had been brought up) a Christian
Jew in Palestine was able to preserve the friendship
and esteem of his unconverted brethren. He was
not regarded as violating any Mosaic law, though
he acknowledged the prophetic character, even the
Messiahship, of Jesus of Nazareth. Those who were
so persuaded might conceivably form a tolerated
sect in Judaism, having in common with the Pharisees
their hope of a resurrection. And so, according to
early ecclesiastical story, James the Just, the first
Christian Bishop of Jerusalem, was able to earn the
respect of his whole nation as an eminently pious

Jew. St Paul (anti-Judaist though he is alleged to be) never condemned this retention of national usages by his brethren in Palestine ; nay (Acts xxi.), James treats as a calumny the assertion that Paul taught Jews residing abroad to abstain from circumcising their children or observing the Mosaic usages. Clearly if these Mosaic usages were given no religious significance, and not supposed to be means necessary to salvation, Paul had no hostility towards them. But it was not found possible long to maintain this attitude of neutrality in mixed congregations. One Christian rite was enough to make it impossible— the common meal, both as used in the Sacrament of the Lord's Supper and in the Love Feast. By eating with men uncircumcised a Jew lost caste. The charge against St Peter after his visit to Cornelius was : " Thou wentest in to men uncircumcised and didst eat with them." And at a later period the same difficulty entangled St Peter again on his visit to Antioch, where, though at first he scrupled not to unite with Gentile Christians in their common feast, he became ashamed of his compliance when there came down visitors (possibly official emissaries) from the Church at Jerusalem, who had never been accustomed to such a breach of Jewish propriety, and to whom it seemed shocking and scandalous.

Our knowledge of the Indian caste system, as I have said, enables us readily to understand the difficulties felt by a Christian Jew on finding himself obliged to mix with Gentiles as brethren and on the most intimate terms. We can understand how a Jew like St Paul who cast off his national

exclusiveness should come to be looked on as having
lost caste, and so to be regarded by unbelieving Jews
as a renegade more deserving of hatred than a
Gentile ; while even Christian Jews could not conquer
their dislike at such laxity, feeling towards it much
as Queen Elizabeth and other non-Romanists did
to a married priesthood. For feelings cannot be
altered in a moment, and the heart will still revolt
at what the intellect can give no good reason for
condemning.

But I should hardly have thought it worth while
to go over all this, if it were not that in order to
grasp the historical position, there are other points
necessary to be apprehended, that yet are unlikely to
occur to a reader of the present day. To us St
Paul's advice commends itself as what would naturally
be given by a man wise and sensible as well as
pious, and as not involving any matter of controversy.
His advice in substance was : Do not trouble yourself
with anxious scrupulosity about the food you eat.
Meat will not make you better or worse. If it has
even been brought into the idol temple it cannot
communicate to you any pollution it may have
received there. But if it appears that your partaking
of these dedicated meats will be construed by your
heathen hosts into homage or adherence to false
gods, or if, though intending no such homage
yourselves, you influence by your example brother
Christians, not so well instructed as yourselves, to
do what to their minds implies adherence to idolatry,
then, what had before been indifferent becomes
unlawful.

You see that this advice takes for granted

that the meat offered to idols has not in itself the power of communicating pollution or causing injury to the recipient, and that if we are bound to abstain, it is not for our own sake but that of others. What is here taken for granted is so heartily conceded by ourselves that we scarcely take notice of the concession. To us the gods of the Greeks and Romans are absolutely nothing—mere figments of the human imagination at a comparatively early period of the progress of our race, but entirely without objective reality. To us it is a mere matter of jesting if we are told of a Christian offering his homage to a statue of Jupiter in the professed hope that the god would gratefully remember it if ever he came into power again. Tolerably sure as we are that the worship of Jupiter and Juno will never revive, we feel even surer of this : that there is no one to be conscious of the adoration offered to their statues, or to feel gratitude for it. Far otherwise was it in the early ages of the Church. We have no direct evidence as to the state of Jewish opinion so early as the days of St Paul, but we have very full evidence as to Jewish opinion in the second century, owing to the preservation of a heretical work, much more Jewish than Christian, the doctrine of which concerning the heathen gods was shared by many of the Christian fathers. In fact, Justin Martyr, one of the earliest Christian writers of whom much remains, was a native of Palestine, where he imbibed this theory of his Jewish countrymen, and by his authority gained acceptance for it from his Christian successors. For the doctrine that the gods of the heathen were no nonentities, but beings powerful to injure, seemed to claim Scripture support.

When the Jews debased themselves by heathen sacrifices, the Psalmist says that they sacrificed their sons and their daughters unto devils. In the context of the present passage St Paul says the things which the Gentiles sacrifice, they sacrifice to devils, or, as it had better be rendered, to demons, and not to God.

The idea of Gentile demon worship suggested by these passages was worked out into a consistent theory. Jupiter and Juno, Venus and Apollo, were all real beings; these might not actually be their right names, but they were the names by which they chose to be known and with which they had made their worshippers acquainted. They belonged to the race of demons, beings, it may be, inferior to angels in power but vastly superior to men. Far down into the middle ages, as many of you know through the "Tannhaüser" legend about Venus, the belief prevailed that the heathen gods were not nonentities but malignant and dangerous demons. The theory of which I speak professed to teach the whole history of these demons. Their origin, it was alleged, dated from the time that the sons of God saw the daughters of men that they were fair, and took them wives of all that they chose. From these unlawful unions sprang a bastard race of giants or demons, in their faculties and powers inheriting some of the superiority to man of their angelic fathers, but debased by their earthly nature and by the wickedness of their origin.[1] These were the beings who gave themselves out as gods, and who very possibly did perpetrate the wicked acts

[1] Clem., *Recog.* i. 29. *Hom.* viii. 13.

are found adopting them, not so long after St Paul's time, were men by no means to be despised—men of good natural gifts, well acquainted with the philosophy of their day, of varied knowledge and considerable intellectual acuteness. Thus you will see that it was by no means the matter of course in Paul's time that it might be now, to teach that dedication in an idol temple made no objective change in the food offered to the heathen divinity, and gave it no power to injure those who partook of it, or to subject them to the demon's power.

At an early stage of the history of Christianity there swept in from the East a great wave of ascetic teaching, which aimed at freeing the soul from the dominion of matter, and of the spirits who ruled over matter. With this end precepts were given— " Touch not, taste not, handle not "; and as it happens in most controversies that men cannot help imbibing some of the ideas even of the men they oppose, some of the principles and some of the superstitions of Gnostic asceticism established themselves in the Church, and held sway there for a considerable time.

But Christianity is entirely free from the charge of having countenanced any of these superstitions. Our Blessed Lord, when asked about certain foods, supposed to be polluting, threw His answer into a pointed form, well adapted to fix itself in the memory of His hearers : " Not that which goeth into the mouth defileth a man, but that which cometh out of the mouth, this defileth a man." St Paul was no personal hearer of our Lord, but this maxim of His could scarcely have been unknown to him, and the

principle it embodies may well have influenced the
advice Paul gave to the Corinthians. By telling
them to eat what was set before them, asking no
questions, he put a direct negative on the notion—
which certainly for a considerable time found ad-
mittance in the Church—of danger of being affected
by noxious influences communicated through the
food by charms or dedications, or other means of
invoking the influence of supernatural hostile powers.

A controversial use has been made of the parallel
which St Paul has drawn between the table of the
Lord and the table of demons to argue from the
analogy of heathen sacrifices to the nature of the
sacrifices of the Christian dispensation. It seems
to me that if any such argument from analogy is
admissible, it may be used to throw light on the
controversy that has been raised as to a real objective presence in the Christian Eucharist. A great
deal of that controversy seems to me purely verbal,
and to have no meaning or significance when once the
old scholastic doctrine about substance and accident has been rejected. All parties agree that consecration makes in the elements no change, of which
the senses can take cognizance ; that all the sensible
qualities remain precisely as before. All parties
agree also that the reception of the consecrated
food does confer spiritual benefit on those who
partake of it worthily, and does involve in deeper
condemnation those who eat and drink unworthily.
It really seems idle therefore to discuss the question
of a presence in the consecrated elements apart
from their reception.

In the Roman Catholic theory this presence is

R

asserted to be in the substance of the consecrated foods, and, if the scholastic theory of substances is held, the assertion of such a presence may have at least some appearance of meaning; but modern philosophy can attach no significance to an assertion about a substance unless something is intended to be asserted about properties by which that substance manifests its presence. Now, the presence in the case we are considering, is owned to be one not manifested by any properties which affect the senses; and as we are speaking of a presence apart from reception, it is not manifested either by any spiritual benefits which affect the soul. Now a presence cognizable neither by body or soul is to my mind a thing so fantastical that I cannot regard it as deserving to be called a real presence.

Yet those who contend for a real objective presence, however open to attack their mode of expressing themselves may be, I believe in real truth are only solicitous for a truth as to which I am in perfect agreement with them. It is this: that the spiritual benefits which all acknowledge follow the worthy receiving of Christ's Holy Sacrament are not to be regarded as the mere result of the soul's action on itself, such as would be the natural consequences of any devout meditation on Christ's death and on the benefits we receive thereby; but that we have a right to believe that through this means of grace which our Lord Himself has appointed, we can have real communion with One outside ourselves to whose direct gift we owe the benefit which we receive. When this has been fully conceded, I ask myself what room for controversy can remain?

The only question I can imagine not purely verbal is, whether or not consecration does not communicate to the elements properties so far independent of the dispositions of the communicant that they would manifest themselves whenever and however received. Thus, according to Roman theory, a priest, if he were wicked enough, might by the uttering of the five sacred words consecrate the loaves in a baker's shop. The same wicked priest might in Church go through the form of consecration, and yet for want of intention the elements might remain common bread and wine. Imagine then the case of two recipients, the one with every worthy disposition communicating in Church of what he believed to be the Lord's Body and Blood, but which in reality had not been consecrated : the other a pious man eating out of Church what he imagined to be common food, but which in reality had been consecrated ; which of these two would eat the Lord's Body and Blood, and would receive the corresponding spiritual benefits ? According to the hypothesis of a real objective change made by consecration it ought to be the second ; but though it cost men no effort to believe this in the ages when this was only one case among many where the magical efficacy of spoken words was universally acknowledged, it is much harder to believe it now, and for my part I freely own that I do not. And it seems to me that if we can at all argue from analogy, we may conclude that St Paul would not have believed it either. For in teaching his converts to eat what was set before them without asking questions, he so entirely puts aside all thought of possible evil influences communicated to their food by previous consecration in an idol temple, that we cannot reasonably think that one who so entirely disbelieved in the possibility of an objective change for evil, would have asserted such a change for good.

I have pursued some of the less obvious thoughts suggested by the text at a length which forbids me now taking up a subject I thought when I began I might have been able to include—the question whether there are limits to our duty of concession to the prejudices of weaker brethren. It is certain that St Paul has taught us both by precept and example to give up some of the liberty that rightfully belongs to us, rather than wound the consciences of others, or tempt them into what they believe to be wrong. Yet if this were pressed too far, it might easily be that the weak would become tyrants over the strong. At the time of the English Reformation it was common with the Puritans, who were dissatisfied with the extent to which it had proceeded, while claiming superiority in spiritual insight to the Church rulers, to claim also the privileges, of weak brethren, and to demand that their objections, whether well founded or not, should be acceded to, lest their conscience, over-scrupulous though it might be, should be offended. And yet if the applicability of St Paul's advice had been admitted, it would hardly have been possible to ordain any rite or ceremony at all. So, again, at the present day the question often presents itself in more forms than one : are we bound to abstain from what, as far as we can judge, is not injurious to ourselves, lest others of less prudence and self-command may be tempted by our example to indulgences which as they use them will not be innocent? The question is evidently too large a one to be taken up now, and perhaps no discussion of it would lead to results in which all could acquiesce. But this at least St Paul may teach us, the duty of looking not every man to his own things but to the things of others. And if there be danger of carrying this principle too far, and in our thought for others doing injustice to our own rightful claims, yet the error is the one into which the fewest are likely to fall, and into which if we do fall we shall have least occasion for self-reproach or regret.

SERMON XXI

THE DAYS OF OUR FATHERS [1]

"We have heard with our ears O God, our fathers have told us what Thou hast done in their time of old : how Thou hast driven out the heathen with Thine hand and planted them in : how Thou hast destroyed the nations and cast them out."
—PSALM xliv. 1, 2.

I SHALL not wonder if many of you are surprised to hear me say that I have for some time looked on this 44th Psalm as one of the most terrible of the Psalms. We are much in the habit of reading the Scriptures, a verse or two at a time ; and those two verses that I have read sound as the appeal of confident, because well justified, faith. "We can trust to Thee for help, because we know what Thou hast done for us in former days : our fathers hoped in Thee, they trusted in Thee, and Thou didst deliver them. They called upon Thee and were holpen ; they put their trust in Thee and were not confounded." And we might expect the Psalm to proceed : "And as our fathers found it so have we ; our faith in the future is justified by our own experience in the past. We too might raise our Ebenezer with the motto : 'Up to this the Lord has helped us.'"

---

[1] Preached in St Patrick's Cathedral, 4th February 1900.

But when we read the Psalm as a whole, we find scarcely a trace of faith or hope; the utterances are of one driven by affliction almost to doubt of God's power or willingness to help. No other Psalm is like this. The 22nd, which I have quoted already, gives as gloomy a picture of the actual condition of the writer; but before the conclusion the clouds have passed away, and the Psalmist can sing praises for deliverance. The 88th Psalm has no such joyful ending, and is uniformly dismal, but suffering has not shattered faith, and the Psalmist can still lay his troubles before God, and still hope to find mercy and deliverance. But in this 44th Psalm the remembrance of happier times is but a sorrow's crown of sorrow. Former deliverances are called to mind, only to be the subject of angry expostulation with the Almighty for having raised hopes and disappointed them. "Often have we been told of Thy mercy to our fathers, for to Thee we ascribed all their successes: it was not their own arm that helped them, but Thy right hand and the light of Thy countenance, because Thou hadst a favour unto them. And so we were confident it would be with us: we did not trust in our bow, nor imagine that our own sword would help us; it was in Thy name only that we put confidence and made our boast of Thee all the day long. Yet what has become of our boasting? Thou goest not forth with our armies. Thou makest us turn our backs upon our enemies, so that they who hate us spoil our goods. And now on account of our mistaken trust in Thee we are laughed to scorn, and held in derision of all that are round about us; we are become a byword unto the heathen, and are filled with shame for the voice of the slanderer and blasphemer. And yet we have not deserved this. If Thou seemest to have forgotten us, we have not forgotten Thee. Though all this has come upon us our heart has not turned back, nor our steps gone out of Thy way. We have not forgotten the name of our God, nor holden up our hands to any strange god. Art Thou no better than one of the gods of the heathen, of whom it could be said, 'Peradventure he sleepeth, and must be awaked.' Wherefore hidest Thou Thy face and forgettest our misery and trouble. Awake, Lord, why sleepest Thou? Awake, and be not absent from us for ever." This is an exceeding great and bitter cry of one pressed above measure beyond his strength—whose faith struggles almost despairingly to make head against the doubts which throng upon it.

As in water face answereth to face, so doth the heart of man to man; and in the Bible, whatever our mood may be, we can seldom fail to find typical examples of one who has passed through the like, from whose history we may draw lessons of encouragement or warning as the case may be. Thus it is well that in our Scripture gallery of portraits we can find patterns of faith in all its stages of growth, from triumph and assurance down to that feeble struggling for life of which the Psalm we have been considering gives a specimen.

We have no means of fixing the date of this Psalm, and therefore we cannot tell how far such faith as the author had was rewarded, or what result he was permitted to see of his expostulations. The

Psalm was evidently written in a time of trouble and of rebuke and of blasphemy; but the Jewish history exhibits many vicissitudes. At times the nation was blessed with victory, and put no limits to their dreams of extension of their dominion over neighbouring peoples. But the sacred historian of the times of the Judges tells us that even at that early period there were vicissitudes. "The people," he says, "forsook the Lord God of their fathers, and provoked Him to anger, and He sold them into the hand of their enemies round about, so that they could no longer stand before their enemies. Nevertheless the Lord raised up judges who delivered them out of the hands of those that spoiled them; for the Lord was with Israel all the days of that judge; but when the judge was dead they corrupted themselves, ceased not from their own doings and from their stubborn way, and again provoked the Lord to anger." You will find a picture of one of those temporary revivals in the 30th Psalm, which is one of thanksgiving for recovery from a state of great anxiety and depression. The Psalmist owns that the trouble had had its origin in the over-confidence generated by long-continued success. "In my prosperity I said, 'I shall never be moved.' Thou, Lord, of Thy goodness hast made my hill so strong. Thou didst turn Thy face from me, and I was troubled. Then cried I unto Thee, O Lord, and gat me to my Lord right humbly." And the result he tells: "Thou hast turned my heaviness into joy: thou hast put off my sackcloth, and girded me with gladness. Sing praises unto the Lord, O ye Saints of His, and give thanks unto Him for a remembrance of His holiness.

For His wrath endureth but the twinkling of an eye, and in His pleasure is life; heaviness may endure for a night, but joy cometh in the morning."

It may be that the great trouble, which the 44th Psalm reveals, was but temporary, and was in like manner succeeded by joyful songs of thanksgiving for deliverance. Whether in that particular case this was so or not we have not been informed; but this we know, that in the end there came heaviness which endured for more than a night, and after which joy did not come in the morning. Their Temple was destroyed: Jerusalem was made a heap of stones. The people had more than ever to complain that they had been made a reproach unto their neighbours, a scorn and derision to them that were round about them. Yet are we to conclude, as some in their despondency were tempted to do, that there was then no overruling Providence? that their God was sleeping, and in spite of all their efforts could not be awaked? We ourselves have learned that our belief that there is a God that ruleth over the kingdom of men need not be shaken because it happens that men have been disappointed in expectations raised through their not having understood the laws by which He works. The Jews, certainly, rightly understood, from what they had read about their ancestors, that men who forsook the pure worship in which they had been trained, and who allowed themselves to be infected by the superstitions of the surrounding heathen, deservedly forfeited the favour of their own God; but they were wrong in concluding that their piety alone must be rewarded with temporal prosperity. It was probably quite true that, as is pleaded in the 44th Psalm, they had not forgotten the name of their God, nor holden up their hands to any strange god. We may believe it to be true, because we know it to be true of the Jews after their return from the Babylonish captivity. Whatever other sins they might have been guilty of, idolatry was not one of them. Never had the nation been so free from tendency that way. Instead of being tempted as their ancestors had been, to seek the favour of the divinities worshipped by the heathen, they prided themselves on their isolation and on their punctilious observance of the law that Moses had given them ; yet instead of being rewarded for their piety by temporal dominion, the little State of returned exiles was no better than a prey to the surrounding kingdoms, to one or other of which it was subjected, until at last, it had, like the rest, to bow to the Roman yoke.

We know now that God's promises of recompense for piety and devotion do not abrogate the general laws by which He rules the world. Those rewards that are designed for greater industry, greater vigilance, greater alertness, careful study, are not taken away for the benefit of the careless or lethargic however pious they may be. We have a notable example that even God's promises are not fulfilled to those who neglect the proper means, in the fact that after Paul had assured his companions in shipwreck that he had received a divine revelation that there should be no loss of life among them, he told them that if they did not prevent the escape of the sailors from the ship they could not be saved. God who rules the course of the world governs it with absolute justice. He is not like some of those earthly sovereigns who will pardon any misdoing if committed by courtiers who pay them compliments. Even those who love Him best must pay the appointed penalty if they transgress any of His laws. As the Psalmist said, "Thou wast a God that forgavest them, though Thou tookest vengeance of their inventions." And those who forget Him are not defrauded of any reward in this life that they have legitimately earned. There is no cause to murmur if we see the wicked in prosperity. They may have legitimately earned what they have got. As our Lord said, "They have their reward."

But these words of His suggest that there may be another reward, which they miss and which others receive. And is it not so? Consider that band of exiles who returned with Ezra and rebuilt their Temple, but in a style so inferior to its predecessor that they who had seen the former wept at the contrast. Yet the glory of the latter Temple was in truth greater than that of the former, however little eyes of earth could recognise it; for its courts were trodden by the feet of the Son of God.

It is not only those that ascribe all their successes to divine protection who delight in recalling to mind the successes won by their ancestors. Equally do those who imagine that it is their own sword or their own bow that hath saved them, pride themselves on the memory of what their fathers have done in days of old, and glory in the thought that such as their history has been in the past such shall it be in the future, and so their empire be of perpetual duration. Such dreams have been entertained by the peoples of all the great monarchies of old, of Egypt, of Assyria, of Babylonia, with whom the wish, "O King, live for ever," was sincerely believed certain to be true, if not of the sovereign, at least of his dynasty; yet their stately palaces, their solemn temples, are now but dust-heaps. And what about the later empire of Rome, whose people fondly counted on immortality for it, and when its poets desired to speak of eternal duration could use such phrases as: "As long as the pontiff and the silent virgin shall ascend the Capitol; or, As long as the house of Æneas shall inherit the immovable rock of the Capitol and the Roman father hold his empire." Departed now alike are the religion and the empire of ancient Rome. And yet we cannot help feeling that it must be otherwise with us, and that our empire, at least, shall last as long as the sun and moon endureth. It is true that an eloquent phrase-maker has ventured to talk of a day when the traveller from New Zealand shall stand on a broken arch of London Bridge to sketch the ruins of St Paul's; yet we cannot persuade ourselves to take such a prediction quite seriously, however our reason may tell us that as no man is endowed with immortality, so neither does any work of his, outliving some others though it may, really endure for ever. And as the individual gets occasional warnings in sickness or in accident that here we have no abiding place, so does a nation at times receive warnings in famines or in pestilences or in defeats before enemies that no earthly prosperity is secure against change. Those vicissitudes of life admonish us to preserve an equal mind, not unduly elated by prosperity nor unduly depressed by adversity. The strongest and healthiest man knows that he holds these blessings by a precarious tenure, and that, however long he may enjoy them, days will come when he shall have no pleasure in them. Yet we count a man a poor creature, who, whenever his health receives a little shake, takes to his bed in low spirits and imagines that he is going to die. And so, too, for a nation. If it is encouraging to think of the successes of our fathers, it is not less so to call to mind their reverses, and to know how they were recovered. It heartens one to bear reverses with fortitude when we can pray, " Oh what troubles and adversities hast Thou shown me ; yet out of all, Thou, Lord, hast delivered me."

I suppose this nation has never been in a sorer strait than it was about a hundred years ago, when it had no ally, and all Europe, under the greatest of leaders, was united against it, when the bank had stopped payment, when the fleet on which our safety depended was in mutiny, and Ireland was in rebellion ; yet our leaders held firm, and out of that war we emerged victorious, and by that time of trial had laid the foundation of England's commercial greatness. Twice before in my own recollection have we had to bear distressing pressure. One was in the Crimean Campaign, when we had to bear months of agonising suspense ; when week after week went on and the besieged city seemed stronger than ever; when day after day we heard new tales of mismanagement and blunders ; when we were pained to hear perpetual accounts of the sufferings endured by our armies, and no progress appeared to be made. Not long after that came the Indian Mutiny, when few of us there were who had not, either in our families or in the household of some friends, the death of some beloved member to mourn, and often under circumstances of such atrocity that we came to hate our enemies with feelings such as we had thought Christians could not be capable of. Yet then, too, we were brought through fire and through water, and came out into a wealthy place; and of that time retain such spirit-stirring memories of bravery and endurance that we could not now wish that the opportunity for exhibition of those qualities had not occurred.

Nor need we murmur, nor deem that God has dealt unlovingly with us, if He has allowed the present war to begin with reverses, and seems as if He regarded those lessons to be the most profitable for us which are taught in the school of adversity. The kind of glory that men are most apt to desire for their nation is such as was gained for France by the first Napoleon, viz., perpetual victory in war, giving a right to dictate the policy of all surrounding peoples, and to levy contributions on them for the benefit of the leading state. But empire of this kind can never be perpetual, for it excites both jealousy and fear; and though a state may be stronger than one or two of its neighbours, it will not be stronger than all together when they come to be united by common apprehension of one too powerful empire. If our national vanity had been gratified by the easy victories on which some sanguine spirits had fondly counted, we should certainly have incurred the reproach from outside spectators of the ill-matched contest, that we had tyrannously used our strength to deprive a weaker neighbour of his liberty and gratify our own sordid greed. And possibly puffed up by success, we might have shown arrogance that would have suggested and justified an attempt to pull down our pride.

But if as yet we have not gained repute for skill in adapting the arts of war to new conditions, is it not both really more honourable to us, and in every way better for us, that the nation should have been given the opportunity of showing calmness under painful trials? And when some of our neighbours expected, as the natural result of our reverses, that we should shriek and scream out that we had been betrayed, we do grateful honour to those who had done their best for us, though unsuccessfully, and brace our energies to the task of turning defeats into triumphs. And if we succeed, as I hope we shall, and when it is seen that we have cheerfully spent millions for which we can expect no financial return, it will be more readily acknowledged that some better motive had inspired our efforts than hope of gain. There was a time when Colonies were valued only as a source of tribute to the mother country. After this hope had been abandoned there came politicians whose chief anxiety was that at least those who had gone away should impose no burden on those who had remained at home; and so if ever a dispute arose between Englishmen and natives of another country, these politicians were anxious to persuade themselves to hold the less expensive opinion that the Englishman must be in the wrong, and the foreigner in the right. I count it to be to our credit that now a different sentiment prevails, and that we own our citizens who have left their home as our brethren whom we will not willingly allow to be enslaved.

It is a worthy object of ambition to strive that this great country of South Africa, which in our century has been opened up to the too rapidly expanding nations of Europe, should be a land of peace ; not showing the spectacle that Europe has exhibited of a land occupied by different nationalities either in actual conflict with each other, or through mutual fears and jealousies forced to spend prodigious sums in military training, in fortresses and armaments ; but inhabited by people though of mixed nationalities yet living in harmony under equal laws, subject to no tribute to distant lands, but with none to make them afraid, cultivating the arts of peace. Contrast the condition of Australia, with its different self-governing provinces peacefully united in a common empire, with what South Africa would become if its inhabitants were divided into hostile camps forced by the necessities of their position into entangling alliances with European nations, and so importing into their midst all the quarrels of Europe ; and you will feel that to gain for that country the happier lot was not too dearly purchased by a war. It was with this object that the American Civil War was waged. In that, too, there was great room for doubt whether the revolters were not, on technical grounds, justified in the step they took ; and in that war, too, those who ultimately triumphed had to contend with great reverses.

S

We know not the future, and cannot tell whether future generations will regard the present period as an epoch of the beginning of a new stage of England's greatness or as the first exhibition of her decline. But one thing we can do—namely, to strive that it shall be a period of which we shall not have cause for shame when our fortitude and energy is compared with that of those who have gone before us. And happy will it be for us if, when we are reminded, as I have reminded you now, of the instability of all human greatness, we learn to draw more closely to Him in every one of Whose dispensations we may find a blessing if we but seek it — and happy if the spectacle of earthly vicissitudes teaches each of us to pray,

> "Change and decay in all around I see,
> O Thou, who changest not, abide with me!"

PRINTED AT THE EDINBURGH PRESS, 9 AND 11 YOUNG STREET.